ON THE PICKLE TRAIL

Monish Gujral is one of India's foremost food writers and columnists, with internationally acclaimed, Gourmand Award-winning cookbooks, several articles in India's leading newspapers and an award-winning food blog. A television personality, having hosted several cookery shows that have aired nationally and internationally, Monish is also the custodian of the Moti Mahal brand. He inherits his passion for culinary integrity from his legendary grandfather, Kundan Lal Gujral, founder of Moti Mahal, who conceived, created and gave the world one of its most beloved cuisines—tandoori—and the famous butter chicken and dal makhani.

On the Pickle Trail

100 RECIPES
from around the World

MONISH GUJRAL

EBURY
PRESS

An imprint of Penguin Random House

EBURY PRESS

USA | Canada | UK | Ireland | Australia
New Zealand | India | South Africa | China

Ebury Press is part of the Penguin Random House group of companies
whose addresses can be found at global.penguinrandomhouse.com

Published by Penguin Random House India Pvt. Ltd
4th Floor, Capital Tower 1, MG Road,
Gurugram 122 002, Haryana, India

First published in Ebury Press by Penguin Random House India 2022

ISBN 9780143453710

Typeset in Adobe Garamond Pro by MAP Systems, Bengaluru, India
Printed at Thomson Press India Ltd, New Delhi

www.penguin.co.in

*To my teacher, guru and inspiration,
my grandfather, Kundan Lal Gujral,
founder of Moti Mahal,
father of tandoori cuisine,
inventor of butter chicken*

CONTENTS

Contents

Contents

Contents

SWEET PRESERVES

FOREWORD

Pickling and Fermentation

Ever think about how people kept food fresh before the modern refrigerator, before the wooden armoire—like the icebox—even before the underground pits filled with snow used by the ancient Greeks, Romans and the Chinese? How did our prehistoric ancestors, especially those living in tropical climates with no access to ice or snow, keep food from spoiling?

The answer is, often they didn't, but instead, they learnt how to control spoilage in a way that allowed rotten food to remain edible—fermentation.

Fermentation is the process by which microbes consume sugars and produce acid, alcohol and gases. Some of the most well-known products of fermentation are wine and beer, where the sugar in the fruit juice or grain is transformed into alcohol by yeast. Similarly, food can also be fermented by bacteria to extend its shelf life. Refrigerators are used much in the same way today, keeping food edible longer. However, the one big drawback is that the modern method of preservation largely excludes microbes from our diet.

Through fermentation, the live bacteria start the digestion process for us. One of the most familiar foods that finds a place in all Indian kitchens is pickles. Pickling is an ancient food preservation technique. But fermented pickles offer much more health benefits than other pickles by acting like probiotics, protecting the body's microbiome and supporting the growth of healthy bacteria in the gut.

When the microbes ferment food, they deplete it of its simple sugars. Too much of simple sugars can cause blood sugar levels to spike, which can lead to health problems, including type 2 diabetes. Bacteria, through fermentation, reduce the simple sugar content of food, making it healthier.

So, the takeaway is that the microbes in fermented food provide two health-promoting functions: reducing the sugar content of the fermented food and interacting with the gut and microbiota. Observations dating back to over a century ago suggest that people who consume a lot of fermented food reap the benefits.

Tanisha Bawa,
certified nutrition coach,
National Academy of Sports Medicine, USA

Certified in advanced gut health from
the Institute for Integrative Nutrition (IIN), USA

AUTHOR'S NOTE

My career in hospitality, spanning thirty years, has made me travel globally in connection with work and led to my interaction with many hospitality experts and international chefs. I was fortunate to meet and learn from some of the greatest master chefs, Michelin star chefs and cuisine innovators. In spite of our diverse nationalities and cultures, we all had the same language—FOOD.

This book is going to be our journey into the tingling world of pickles. *On the Pickle Trail* documents the pickles of many countries. The purpose of writing this book is to encourage the liberal use of pickled food in our daily diet as it is healthy to eat pickles. I would also like to promote home artisanal cooking which most of us are forgetting about, due to the charms of the online retail world. We remember our grandmothers or mother making pickles or cooking our favourite dishes with love. Every family has its own unique recipes, which are close to their heart, as the flavours and comfort that these dishes bring to us are priceless.

At this point, I'd like you to remember that Moti Mahal restaurants innovated the pickled onions called sirka pyaaz (onions in vinegar) which became the trendsetter, adopted by all Indian restaurants across the globe.

This book will not only take us back to our roots but will revive the art of making pickles at home, rather than buying processed pickles with fancy labels from supermarkets, which are pasteurized for longer shelf life but destroy the naturally occurring probiotics.

Pickles are usually fermented, which aids digestion and improves gut health, besides making food tasty and easily available in all seasons. Fermentation as a process precedes human history. It is the conversion of sugars and other carbohydrates into alcohol or other preservative organic acids and carbon dioxide. The by-products of fermentation can also be used for human consumption. Fermented fruit juices yield wine, grains are made into beer and when potatoes are fermented and then distilled, we get vodka and gin. Carbon dioxide is used to leaven bread and produce organic acids that help in preserving fruits and vegetables. Fermentation, in short, enriches our diet as it diversifies the flavours and textures of food, preserves food and enhances food substrates with proteins and essential amino acids. Fermented foods are rich in probiotic bacteria that help in digestion and enhance the immune system, which is much required in our modern-day lifestyles.

Welcome to the pickle trail. Let's start pickling.

TABLE OF MEASURES

1 cup = 225 ml
1 tsp = 5 ml
1 tbsp = 3 tsp
A pinch = ⅛ tsp (literally a pinch)
A dash = 1–2 drops

STERILIZATION OF JARS

In a large, deep pot, immerse the jars and lids in hot water. Bring the water to a boil and continue to boil for 15 minutes with a lid on the pot.

Turn off the heat and let the jars remain in the pot.

Just before pickling, remove from the water with cooking tongs and invert the jars on a clean kitchen towel or a clean rack to dry.

HOME CANNING PROCESS

Sterilize the glass Mason jars.

Fill in the desired pickle and pour hot brine up to the rim leaving about ½ inch space at the top.

Tap and shake the jar a little to release air bubbles, if any, as these will spoil the pickle.

Seal the jar tightly with a non-reactive lid.

Process the jars under a hot water bath for about 10 minutes.

Remove the jars and let them cool to room temperature.

Store the jars in a cool, dry place and let the pickle ferment as per your taste.

PICKLE SPICES

1 PICKLING SPICE

Ingredients

½ tsp cinnamon powder
½ tsp ground cloves
¼ tsp ground nutmeg
2 tbsp mustard seeds
1 tbsp coriander seeds
2 whole cloves
1 tsp ground ginger
1 tsp red pepper flakes, crushed
1 bay leaf, crumbled
1 2-inch cinnamon stick

Method

Place mustard seeds, all-spice powder (see page 6), coriander seeds and pepper flakes in a glass jar and give it a shake.

Add ground ginger and crumbled bay leaf and shake again. Place cinnamon stick on top and seal the jar tightly.

Store it for a month.

2 CAJUN SPICE

Ingredients

2 tsp salt
2 tsp garlic powder
2 tsp paprika
1 tsp ground black pepper
1 tsp onion powder
1 tsp cayenne pepper
1¼ tsp dried oregano
½ tsp red pepper flakes
1 tsp dried thyme

Method

Mix together salt, garlic powder, paprika, black pepper, onion powder, cayenne pepper, oregano, red pepper flakes and thyme until evenly blended.

Store in an airtight container.

3 ALL-SPICE POWDER

Ingredients

1 tbsp ground cinnamon
1 tbsp ground cloves
1 tbsp ground nutmeg

Method

Mix all the ingredients and store in an airtight container.

4 CURRY POWDER

Ingredients

2 tbsp ground coriander
2 tbsp ground ginger
2 tbsp ground black pepper
2 tbsp cinnamon powder
2 tbsp ground cardamom
2 tbsp cumin powder

Method

Mix all together and store in an airtight container.

5 PANCH PHORON MASALA

In Bengali, *panch* means 'five' and *phoron* means 'tempering'. As the name suggests, it is a blend of five aromatic seeds, which are tempered in oil to add a lovely aroma to the dish.

Ingredients

1 tbsp cumin seeds
1 tbsp nigella seeds
1 tbsp mustard seeds
1 tbsp fennel seeds
1 tbsp fenugreek seeds

Method

Mix all together and store in an airtight jar.

PICKLES FROM AROUND THE WORLD

1
GIARDINIERA
(ITALIAN PICKLED VEGETABLES)

In Italian, the word *giardiniera* means 'female gardener' or 'from the garden'. As the name suggests, the bouquet of vegetables, such as peppers, carrots, cauliflower, zucchini and onions pickled with either red or white wine vinegar, some salt, red pepper flakes, garlic and herbs like oregano, can be aptly termed 'garden salad'.

The pickle is also popular in Chicago where it was introduced by Italian immigrants. Italians enjoy giardiniera as antipasti with a variety of cheese, crackers and raw meats or with salads. However, in the US, the salad is usually eaten as relish with hot dogs, burgers, pizzas, pasta, etc.

I simply enjoy eating it with my multigrain kebab sandwich and, interestingly, with any biryani or kebabs. Just try it; you will love this simple, delicious salad.

Ingredients

1 red bell pepper
1 yellow bell pepper
5 medium carrots
½ cup oil-preserved seedless olives
4 celery ribs
1 bunch parsley, chopped
5 cups cauliflower florets
¾ cup red chilli peppers
2 tsp fennel seeds

For pickling brine

3½ cups water
½ cup olive oil
¾ cup sugar (I personally use brown sugar although, traditionally, you can use granulated white sugar)
2⅔ cups distilled white wine vinegar
4½ tbsp kosher salt or pink Himalayan salt
1 tsp yellow mustard seeds
1 tsp red pepper flakes
1 tsp oregano
2 bay leaves

Method

Cut all the vegetables into 1-inch pieces, other than the cauliflower, which will be used as florets.

In a pan, bring all the pickling brine ingredients to a boil over medium heat.

Add sugar and bay leaves.

Remove from heat and bring it to room temperature.

In a separate bowl, boil 20–25 cups of water.

Add cauliflower to the boiling pot.

Cook for about 4–5 minutes and remove.

Repeat the same process for vegetables other than celery and carrots, which are to be cooked for 2 minutes only.

Drain the water and spread the vegetables on a clean kitchen towel. Let them cool down to room temperature.

In a glass jar, add red chilli peppers and olives to the pickling liquid along with salt, red pepper flakes, oregano, fennel seeds, mustard seeds and olive oil.

Add all the vegetables, making sure all are submerged in the brine.

Chill for a day in the fridge.

Keep refrigerated until consumed.

2 L'HAMD MARKAD (MOROCCAN PRESERVED LEMONS)

As in every culture, Moroccans too pickled lemons to preserve the fruit once the growing season passed. Preserved lemons are an integral part of Moroccan kitchens. Traditionally, this pickle is made with lemons and kosher salt; however, there are many variations depending upon the choice of condiments that can be added to the pickle.

Moroccan preserved lemons have a unique taste. My favourite is the one made with kosher salt only, as it retains the tanginess and original flavour of the lemons. If you are in Morocco, use citron lemons, and if elsewhere, any lemon variety will do.

I met a Moroccan student while I was teaching at Le Cordon Bleu in Paris, who gave me this recipe and we made it in the class. After five weeks, we ate it with hot, crispy, mouth-watering samosas, which I had taught them in the class.

Ingredients

12 citron or any available variety of lemons
½ cup kosher salt
1 tsp brown sugar
1 tsp rock salt
½ cup freshly squeezed lemon juice

Method

Make a deep cross incision in the lemons, ensuring that they do not separate at the bottom.

Mix together kosher salt, rock salt and brown sugar.

Pry the lemons open and fill in the kosher salt abundantly.

Put 2 tbsp of the salt mixture in the jar and start placing the lemons in it.

Press them down so that the lemon juice is extracted and the juice covers the lemons till the top.

Add additional lemon juice to cover the lemons.

Add salt, rock salt and brown sugar on the top and seal the jar with the lid.

Let it sit for a few days, turning the jar upside down occasionally so that all the lemons are uniformly soaked in the juice.

Open the lid every 2 days and press the lemons to ensure more juice is extracted.

Repeat the process for a week, then let the lemons lie for 4–5 weeks until the lemon rind is soft and the bitterness has gone.

Refrigerate the lemons in the jar until consumed.

3 KYURI ASA-ZUKE (JAPANESE PICKLED CUCUMBERS)

Although pickled ginger may be the most popular Japanese pickle globally, kyuri asa-zuke, a slightly salted and pickled cucumber is the most popular throughout Japan.

I was introduced to this pickle in Tokyo when I had gone for the launch of my book *On the Kebab Trail* on invitation by the Indian Embassy a few years ago.

The pickle can be served in thin slices as a condiment and can be used in sandwiches, as garnish on pizzas and burgers, and alongside the main course.

I love to have this simple pickle rolled up in pita along with herbed feta and a drizzling of extra virgin olive oil.

Ingredients

4 seedless Japanese cucumbers (350–400 gm)
4 tsp granulated sea salt
⅓ tsp dried wakame (dried seaweed), chopped and soaked in warm water for 10 minutes

1 tsp granulated sugar
2 tbsp rice vinegar
8 tbsp water
1 tbsp soya sauce
1 tsp roasted sesame seeds

Method

Wash the cucumbers and pat dry.

Rub the cucumbers with salt, cut them into ½ inch slices and place them in a clean, sterilized jar.

Press them to fit into the jar.

Sprinkle the seaweed over them.

Mix all other ingredients in a bowl and pour over the cucumbers.

Cover the rim with a non-reactive lid.

Place the jar in the refrigerator overnight, occasionally turning it upside down.

Keep refrigerated until consumed.

4 TORSHI LEFT (ISRAELI TURNIP PICKLE)

In Hebrew, *torshi* means 'pickle' or 'sour' and *left* means 'the most forgotten vegetable'—such as turnip.

It's a simple pickle to make and one can enjoy it as a relish and with the main course, and also with salads. The turnips are fermented in brine made with vinegar and kosher salt, spices and a beet, rendering a unique pink turnip pickle.

Torshi, also pronounced *turshi*, is a Middle-Eastern pickle made by a process where salt is the key ingredient to preserve food such as vegetables, fruits, fish, meats, etc. Arabs mostly use vinegar to make pickles, whereas Jews also use red wine vinegar since they don't have liquor restrictions. The variations of torshi left also have inclusions of pomegranate, dates, raisins, apples and grains along with turnips.

Although I have never travelled to Israel and it's on my bucket list, I learnt this recipe from a Jewish friend in the US who was studying to be a chef in New York. He told me that this recipe was from his native town and as a family tradition, they would eat it with stew and bread.

Ingredients

1 kg white turnips
4 garlic cloves
1 tsp pink peppercorns
Stalk of celery, chopped
1 raw beetroot, peeled and cut into small pieces
3 tbsp salt
1 whole dry red chilli
1 cup water
1 cup white vinegar

Method

Dissolve salt in water, add vinegar and bring it to a boil.

Wash and peel the turnips and pat dry.

Cut the turnips and beetroot in medium pieces and put them in a clean, dry glass jar.

Add garlic, peppercorns, chilli and the chopped celery stalk.

Pour in the salty brine till the rim, ensuring that the turnips are fully immersed.

Seal the jar tightly with the glass lid.

Store at room temperature for about 10 days and thereafter in the refrigerator until consumed.

5 KIMCHI
(SOUTH KOREAN VEGETABLE PICKLE)

One of my favourite pickles. I remember going for Chinese meals with my family to a restaurant where they would serve the pickle complimentary as most Chinese restaurants do. Many a time, I would eat only kimchi as a starter.

Kimchi is a famous traditional Korean side dish or pickle made with fermented vegetables, mainly cabbage, radish and spring onions seasoned with salt and a hint of garlic. It's a Korean national dish and an average Korean consumes about 40 pounds of kimchi per annum.

It makes a perfect side dish and relish for burgers and sandwiches too.

Ingredients

2 kg cabbage
1 radish, shredded
3 green onions, chopped

4 garlic cloves, pressed
1 tsp black pepper
½ cup rice vinegar
2 tsp soya sauce
2 tsp caster sugar
2 tsp sea salt
1 tsp ground ginger
2 tbsp virgin olive oil

Method

Clean and pat dry all vegetables.

Chop and shred all vegetables.

Finely cut the garlic and ginger.

In a bowl, put all the condiments along with olive oil, vinegar, soya sauce and sugar, and add in garlic and ginger.

Put all in a blender and blend into a smooth mixture.

Place all the vegetables in a serving dish and pour the mixture over it.

Place in the refrigerator to retain its crispy texture and serve chilled.

6 SWEDISH PICKLED HERRING

Due to exceptionally long and extreme winters in Northern Europe, pickling has been an intrinsic part of North European cuisine. Swedes, too, have been pickling since the Middle Ages to preserve food.

Herring was considered poor man's food in Swedish culture due to its abundance. However, it became popular later and was eaten with vodka. Today, pickled herring is a delicacy and no Swedish smorgasbord is complete without it. It has a prominent place on the Swedish dinner table during festivals like Christmas and Easter.

The basic version of pickled herring combines salt, vinegar, condiments, cranberries, oranges and strawberries, among other ingredients. Pickled herring can be eaten with boiled eggs, sour cream and jacket potatoes and, of course, with the main course as well.

It can be made with many variations, where one can add dill, mustard, tomatoes, onions, pitted olives, prunes, etc.

Try it with rye bread, liberally spread with feta, pesto and olive oil, topped with the pickled herring, and you are sure to relish it.

Ingredients

4 herring fillets
¼ cup kosher salt
½ cup distilled white wine
½ cup water
4 cups water for boiling
¼ cup sugar
2–3 cloves
1 tsp brown sugar
1 small white onion, sliced
2 bay leaves
1 tsp peppercorns
1 tsp mustard seeds
2 tsp all-spice powder (recipe on page 6)
1 lemon, thinly sliced

Method

Heat 4 cups water and add salt. Bring to room temperature.

Submerge the herring fillets and let it rest overnight in the refrigerator.

Add ½ cup water, wine, sugars, all-spice powder, bay leaves, peppercorns, mustard seeds, cloves and sliced onion in a bowl and bring it to a boil.

Remove from heat and bring to room temperature.

Add lemon slices.

Add pieces of herring fillet to the brine; then place it in a sterilized glass jar and seal it.

Let it rest for 24 hours before consuming.

Store in the refrigerator for up to 1 month.

7 GERMAN SAUERKRAUT

Highly popular in Germany, this pickle was actually invented by the Chinese. The Chinese pickled the cabbage in rice wine. In Germany, the pickling process followed is called lacto-fermentation, which imparts a delightfully sour flavour to the crunchy pickle.

All fruits and vegetables have good bacteria called lactobacillus on their surface. When they are submerged in brine, the bacteria begin to convert the sugar in fruits and vegetables into lactic acid, which is a natural preservative and prevents the growth of any harmful bacteria. This process has been used for centuries to preserve fruits and vegetables.

Sauerkraut contains healthy probiotics such as you'd find in a bowl of Greek yoghurt. It is normally eaten layered between sandwiches, wraps or even burgers, and also with stews, pork chops, duck, etc.

It is one of the easiest pickles to make, as you just have to combine salt with shredded cabbage and a little water. In the process, the cabbage releases its own moisture, creating its own brining solution. There are many variations, though. One may add juniper berries, blackcurrants or vine leaves for additional flavour.

Ingredients

1 large head of cabbage
2 tbsp kosher salt
1 tbsp caraway seeds for flavouring
2 vine leaves

Clean glass Mason jar
Clean marble or weights to press the cabbage down in the jar
Cloth for covering the jar

Method

Slice and shred the cabbage.

Combine salt with caraway seeds and rub thoroughly on the cabbage.

The process will take about 10 minutes until the cabbage starts releasing its moisture and becoming limp.

Mix in the caraway seeds and vine leaves.

Press the treated cabbage in the sterilized jar and compress with weights.

Just in case the cabbage is not fully submerged, add some water with salt.

Cover the rim of the jar with a porous cloth tightly held in place with a band.

Shake the jar every few hours for the next 24 hours and keep pressing the cabbage down.

Store in a cool and dark room for 3–8 days or until you feel you like the taste.

Remove the weights and the cloth. Cover with the lid of the jar and refrigerate.

You can enjoy the pickle for months.

8 CORNICHONS
(FRENCH PICKLED GHERKINS)

Cornichons are also known as gherkins in English. These are crisp mini cucumbers with a bumpy surface. The tart and crunchy pickle is made with little finger-size gherkins and is used as an appetizer with meats, fish eggs, sandwiches, burgers, or as a cheeseboard accompaniment.

I am a huge fan of gherkins as a snack. I often pull out a few gherkins from the jar and just eat them with feta cheese and olives while watching television. It's a hearty snack and ensures one doesn't gain any weight.

Ingredients

500 gm cornichons/gherkins
2 bay leaves
1 tbsp sugar
1 tbsp fresh dill
1 garlic bulb, peeled and halved

2 cloves
1 tsp black peppercorns
1 cup water
½ medium white onion, sliced
1 cup distilled white vinegar
¼ cup kosher salt

Method

In a large bowl, toss the gherkins with salt.

Allow the salt to absorb and draw the moisture from the gherkins.

Spread them on a paper kitchen towel for about 2 hours.

In a pan, add vinegar, water, sugar and the remaining salt, and bring to a boil on medium heat for about 8 minutes.

Place the gherkins, peppercorns, cloves, garlic, dill and onion in a sterilized jar and fill it with the hot pickling solution, leaving some head space in the jar.

Seal the jar tightly with its lid and give it a little shake to mix well.

If you have a canner, then process it for 10 minutes in boiling water or give the jar a warm water bath for 10 minutes.

Store in a dark place for about 4 weeks before consuming.

Once open, refrigerate until consumed.

9 AMERICAN DILL PICKLE

Cucumber pickles are popular all over the world. However, all countries have their own version of this simple and popular pickle.

It's simple because you can make it in 30 minutes at home, and popular as it can be used as a snack, in sandwiches, burgers, relishes and salads.

Americans claim sour cucumber pickle in vinegar and dill seeds is their own invention or national pickle.

I love to eat it with vegetable cutlets dipped in sour cream, squeezed in pita bread and with mint sauce—the taste is divine.

Try it at home and you will remember me while eating it.

Ingredients

1 kg cucumber (preferably Persian)
1 cup water
2 tsp dill seeds

⅓ tsp red chilli flakes
1 cup apple cider vinegar
2 tbsp kosher salt or pink Himalayan salt
4 garlic cloves, smashed
1 tbsp sugar
1 tsp mustard seeds
1 tsp coriander seeds

Method

Wash and dry the cucumbers. Trim the ends as the tips have enzymes that make the cucumbers limp. Cut them into thin spears.

Pour vinegar and water in a non-reactive pan, add salt and bring to a boil over medium heat.

Stir in the rest of the ingredients other than cucumbers.

Stuff the cucumbers in the jar and pour the brine mixture over this.

Pack the cucumbers lightly, seeing that they are not compressed, leaving ½ inch space at the top.

Screw the lid on tightly.

Shake and turn around the jar to release air bubbles.

Keep it in a cool, dark place for 48 hours and then refrigerate for use.

Canning is advisable if you want to store them for a longer time.

10 GARI
(JAPANESE GINGER PICKLE)

The first item one thinks of when one visits a Japanese restaurant is the thinly sliced, sweet and delicious pink marinated ginger. The Japanese use younger ginger and marinate it with a vinegar and sugar solution to make gari.

Gari is not only used as palate cleanser after sushi but also aids digestion. Gari is also called sushi ginger and it is one of the most inexpensive and simple pickles to make. While younger ginger is tender and can be pickled immediately on peeling, the dry mature ginger needs to be peeled and rubbed with salt to make it tender.

I remember in my childhood home, my granny would pickle ginger, lemons and green chilli, which were always part of any meal, be it breakfast, lunch, evening tea with savouries and, of course, dinner.

Ingredients

250 gm ginger
1 tbsp kosher salt
½ cup rice vinegar
¾ cup water
1 tbsp granulated sugar

Method

Prepare a glass Mason jar and keep it dry.

Peel the ginger and cut into thin slices.

Rub the ginger with salt and set aside for about an hour.

Place ginger in the jar.

In a bowl, mix vinegar, water and sugar and bring it to a boil on medium heat.

Pour the brine in the jar over the ginger, leaving about an inch space on the top.

Tap the jar to remove the air bubbles and then seal it tightly with the lid.

Bring to room temperature and refrigerate for about 36–48 hours before use.

Keep in the refrigerator once the lid is opened until consumed.

11 INLAGDA RÖDBETOR (SCANDINAVIAN BEET PICKLE)

It is one of the favourite Scandinavian pickles, made with beetroots, vinegar, sugar and salt solution, with caraway seeds or cloves as per taste.

Soon after the award ceremony held at the Frankfurt Book Fair, where my book, *The Moti Mahal Cookbook*, was awarded as the best of the best cookbooks among the best of Gourmand-awarded books in the last twenty years, I was invited by a few chefs in Scandinavia for a culinary trip. I was introduced to the finest Scandinavian restaurants and chefs and, of course, Swedish cuisine. It was here in Sweden that I tasted this simple but delicious pickle, besides many Swedish delicacies. It is one of my very favourite places in Northern Europe.

I have fond memories of my various trips to Sweden. Having many foodie friends there, a few having upscale restaurants, it has been a wonderful insight to the food culture of Sweden. Nordic cuisine and cooking techniques are not only unique but very flavourful. From reindeer meat, truffles and wild berries to celebrated chefs and their exotic style of cooking, Sweden has always influenced my style of cooking. Sweden, like the rest of Northern Europe, has harsh winters, which has prompted Swedes to preserve their food, which includes pickling.

Pickled beetroots are a classic Swedish dish. For pickling, Swedes normally use a solution called ättika, a solution of acetic acid in water.

Ingredients

4 medium beets
2–3 cloves
3 cups apple cider vinegar
1 cup water
¾ cup granulated sugar (I usually use brown sugar as it is more healthy)
1 whole red chilli pepper

Method

Wash the beets.

In a bowl, add water and cook the unpeeled beets till tender.

Drain and cool to room temperature.

Prepare a glass jar.

Peel the beets once cooled and cut them into thin slices.

Put them in the jar with the cloves and chilli pepper.

In a bowl, mix vinegar, water and sugar and bring it to a boil.

Pour the pickling brine into the jar over the beets.

Keep an inch space at the top and tap the jar to remove the bubbles.

Seal and store for 3–4 weeks before using.

Once opened, refrigerate it until consumed.

12 THE UK'S PICKLED EGGS

This is my all-time favourite pickled snack. It's so versatile that one can eat it with a main course or as a snack. I love it with my beer and, occasionally, I use it in my salads too.

Normally, eggs are piled and pickled in vinegar and salt brine, but there are many versions. One can add beets, onions, spices, jalapeños or mustard as per choice.

I love to add pickled beets with some cinnamon as it imparts a beautiful pink colour to the eggs.

Ingredients

8 hard-boiled eggs, peeled
1 cup beet juice
1 cup apple cider vinegar
2 tbsp granulated sugar (I use brown sugar)
1 star anise
1 clove
2 cardamom pods

1 bay leaf
1 tsp mustard powder
2 jalapeños

Method

Peel the eggs and place them in a clean, dry glass jar.

In a non-reactive pan, boil vinegar, beet juice, sugar, spices and condiments.

Bring to room temperature.

Pile the eggs in the jar along with jalapeños.

Pour the pickling brine over the eggs leaving 1 inch space at the top. Tap the jar to remove the bubbles and seal with the lid.

The eggs will be red in a few days. However, if they sit longer, the pink colour will penetrate inside the egg core too.

You can refrigerate it up to a month once it is opened.

13 CEBOLLAS ENCURTIDAS (ECUADORIAN PICKLED ONIONS)

This is particularly close to my heart, since my grandfather, who invented butter chicken and tandoori cuisine, popularized the whole small red onions in vinegar trend at Moti Mahal, which is an all-time favourite of all diners at our restaurants, till date.

The South American–Ecuador version is easy and mostly accompanies tacos, burgers, nachos and grills.

Enjoy the pickle as a side dish or accompaniment or on cheeseboards and meze.

Ingredients

3 medium red onions, thinly sliced
1 tbsp kosher salt
½ cup apple cider vinegar
1 cup warm water
1 tbsp granulated sugar (I use brown sugar)

1 medium ripe beet (optional)
2 red chilli peppers, whole

Method

Slice the onions and put them in a glass jar.

In a non-reactive pan, heat vinegar, water, salt and sugar along with peeled and sliced beet.

Pour the solution into the jar and add onions and red peppers.

Leave an inch of space at the top, ensuring that the onions are completely immersed in the brine.

Let them sit for an hour before sealing it.

Tap the jar to remove the bubbles. Seal the jar with its lid.

Keep them in the fridge for 24–48 hours or more as per your palate.

They can be stored for a month in the fridge.

14 TSUKEMONO
(JAPANESE MIXED VEGETABLE PICKLE)

In Japan, it's customary to serve pickles with meals. The pickled vegetables are called tsukemono. Since vegetables are hard to find in winters in Japan, pickling has gained importance.

There are many versions of tsukemono: one can make it with single vegetables like cabbage or with a mix of vegetables like ginger, cucumber, Chinese cabbage, radish, etc. You could even have an infusion of certain fruits in a brine made of soy, rice wine vinegar, water, sugar and salt.

Vegetable pickles are popular in Japan due to the Buddhist community there, who are primarily vegetarian.

This is a simple, light and delightful pickle, and one can experiment with a choice of vegetables, berries and fruits that one likes.

I normally add pineapple and green apple thinly sliced in my tsukemono, which imparts an earthy twist to the pickle.

Ingredients

1 cup Chinese cabbage
3 turnips
3 radishes
1 bunch green grapes
1¼ cup pineapple, thinly sliced
1 daikon
1 cup soy sauce (Shoyu)
1 cup Japanese cooking wine
1 cup plain rice vinegar
Kosher salt to taste
1 tbsp red pepper flakes

Method

Cut the turnips and radishes in quarters.

Shred the cabbage and peel the daikon, and cut it into quarter moons.

Cut the pineapple as mentioned in the ingredients list.

Rub all the vegetables with salt and set aside for 20 minutes.

Squeeze extra water from the vegetables.

In a bowl, mix soy sauce, rice vinegar, red pepper flakes and plain rice vinegar.

Put the vegetables and fruits in a jar fully immersed in the pickling brine and keep it for at least 4–5 days.

Refrigerate until consumed. It can be stored for 4 weeks.

15 PIKLIZ
(HAITIAN PICKLED RELISH)

Haitian cuisine, with its African and French influences along with traces of Indian and Spanish fare, is very interesting, as it is a melting pot of various cuisines. In Haiti, one can savour Indo–African, Afro–French and even Afro–Spanish fusion cuisine, besides local food.

Hot peppers, mangoes, avocados, grapefruits, sugarcane, okra, mushrooms and various meats are available all across the country.

Haitian pickled relish, called pikliz (pronounced 'pickles'), is a fiery, bright Haitian condiment served with the main course, meats, sandwiches and salads, among others.

Ingredients

1 cup carrot juliennes
6 scotch bonnet peppers, sliced
2 cups cabbage, thinly sliced

½ cup shallots, thinly sliced
1 red bell pepper, sliced
5 cloves
1½ tsp kosher salt
2½ cups distilled white vinegar
2 tbsp fresh lemon juice
8–10 whole black peppers (optional) to impart a slightly earthy flavour

Method

Put all the vegetables on a tray and rub salt evenly on them.

In a non-reactive pan, heat water, distilled vinegar and salt. Bring it to a boil and simmer for 10 minutes.

Pile all the vegetables in a sterilized glass Mason jar and add cloves, lemon juice and black peppers.

Fill the jar with pickling brine till the rim.

Tap a little to remove the bubbles.

Ensure all the vegetables are immersed in brine and there is an inch of space at the top before sealing the jar.

Let it rest for 4–5 days before serving, making sure to shake the jar a couple of times a day until ready.

Refrigerate until consumed.

16 JALAPEÑOS EN ESCABECHE (MEXICAN PICKLED JALAPEÑO PEPPERS)

I love spice and who doesn't like a little spice and flavours in their food or life?

During my visit to Rio, I met a Mexican chef in the hotel I was staying at, who taught me this simple but flavourful recipe of pepper pickle. This is one of my all-time favourites, as it is quite versatile; one can eat it with salads, sandwiches, burgers, pasta and even meats.

I often add a bowl of jalapeño peppers on my cheeseboard along with olives, gherkins and crackers. Brush the cracker with cream cheese and add this pickle; it really tastes yummy.

Classic pickled jalapeños or escabeche are made with fresh jalapeño peppers, carrot, onions, garlic and some herbs.

Ingredients

500 gm jalapeño peppers

1 red bell pepper, sliced
2 white onions, sliced
2 medium carrots, peeled and sliced in diskettes
1 head of garlic, peeled but not severed
4 cups apple cider vinegar or distilled white vinegar
2 cups of water
2½ tbsp kosher salt
1 tsp dried Italian oregano
3 sprigs thyme
2 bay leaves
1 tbsp granulated sugar
⅓ cup virgin olive oil to fry

Method

Clean and dry a Mason jar.

Cut the stems of the peppers and make a lengthwise incision.

Fry all vegetables over medium heat for about 7–8 minutes.

In a non-reactive pot, heat the water, sugar, salt and vinegar. Bring it to a boil on medium heat. Let it simmer for about 10 minutes.

Mix in the seasoning.

Pile all the vegetables in the Mason jar.

Pour the hot pickling brine over the vegetables till the rim, ensuring all the vegetables are well immersed.

Shake and seal the jar. Let it rest for 4–5 days.

Once opened, refrigerate until consumed.

17 SIRKA PYAAZ (INDIAN VINEGAR ONIONS)

I have grown up eating this pickle. It was popularized by my grandfather, Kundan Lal Gujral, at Moti Mahal, and adopted by every North Indian restaurant, which served it as an accompaniment. Vinegar onions are crisp, besides being sweet and sour.

Ingredients

20 small round pearl onions
1 medium beetroot, diced
¼ cup sugar
1 tsp salt
1 cup white vinegar
3 cups water

Method

In a bowl, mix water and vinegar, and add sugar till dissolved.

Add onions, beetroot and salt.

Stir well.

Empty in a sterilized jar and fill the brine to immerse the onions fully.

Add more vinegar if needed.

Store in a cool, dark place for 2–3 days and then serve.

Refrigerate until consumed.

18 ALASKAN SALMON PICKLE

Alaska ranks as one of the world's best and healthiest fisheries. Alaskan king salmon is a great tasting fish and weighs up to 40 pounds. Likewise, the pickle made from Alaskan salmon is tasty and popular all over the world.

Ingredients

1 kg Alaskan salmon, skinned and deboned, cut in small cubes
1 cup sea salt
4 tbsp kosher salt
2 cups white vinegar
¼ cup olive oil
¼ cup coriander seeds
6 peppercorns
¼ tsp pickling spice (recipe on page 3)
3 garlic cloves, thinly sliced
¼ cup granulated sugar

8 orange slices
12 slices boiled beets
8 dill sprigs
2 jalapeños, cut in discs

Method

Place the salmon cubes in a pan, rub sea salt on them and refrigerate for about an hour.

Remove and wash in cold water to remove the salt.

In a pan, boil water, vinegar, garlic, spices, salt, coriander seeds, peppercorns, olive oil and sugar for 10 minutes and remove from heat.

In a pan full of water, cook salmon for about 2 minutes and remove from water.

In a sterilized jar, layer the salmon with oranges, beets, jalapeños and dill.

Cover with pickling brine and seal with the lid.

Refrigerate for 48 hours before use. It can be used up to 7 days only.

19 ACAR KETIMUN (INDONESIAN CUCUMBER PICKLE)

Cucumbers are always welcome in salads, detox juices, sandwiches, burgers and with the main course. This refreshing pickle caught my attention while I was travelling in the country, because of its simplicity and flavour. The pickle is usually served with grilled foods as a side dish.

Ingredients

1 fresh cucumber, thickly sliced
1 white onion, thinly sliced
2 tbsp fresh parsley
2 tbsp sugar
1 tsp kosher salt
4 peppercorns
2 cloves
1 bay leaf
1 cup distilled white vinegar

½ tsp crushed red pepper
1 whole red chilli pepper

Method

In a non-reactive pan, add all vegetables with vinegar, condiments and seasoning, except cucumber and parsley.

Bring it to a boil on medium heat and cook for about 8 minutes.

Stir in cucumber and parsley.

Remove from heat and set aside for an hour to bring to room temperature.

Pour in a sterilized Mason glass jar, seal the lid tightly and allow fermenting overnight.

Refrigerate after opening. The pickle can be served for a week.

20 CEBOLLAS ENCURTIDAS (MEXICAN PICKLED RED ONIONS)

A very simple and quick pickle recipe—you may make it faster than you can read this recipe.

One can pair it with grills, salads, burgers, pastas, etc.

Ingredients

2 large red onions, thinly sliced
8 peppercorns, coarsely ground
½ tsp cumin seeds
1 large red chilli pepper
1 tsp dried oregano
1 tsp kosher salt
2 cups apple cider vinegar
2 bay leaves
4 garlic cloves
1 tsp sugar

Method

In a non-reactive pan, heat the vinegar along with pepper, peppercorns, cumin, oregano, bay leaves, garlic, sugar and salt.

In a jar, put the sliced onions and pour the vinegar mixture until they are fully immersed.

Rest overnight until onions turn bright pink.

Store in the fridge for up to 2 weeks.

21 INDONESIAN ACAR

Acar simply means 'pickle'. This is an easy recipe made with chopped cucumber, carrots, shallots and bird's eye chillies pickled in vinegar, spices and sweetened with sugar. It is usually served as a side dish with any main dish, including Indonesian fried rice, fried noodles, satay, martabak or soto.

Ingredients

2 cucumbers, remove the seeds and cut into cubes
3 carrots, peeled and cut into cubes
1 shallot, peeled and cut into cubes
2 red chillies
3 tbsp water
4 tbsp sugar
2 tsp sea salt
1 cup rice vinegar

Method

Cut the vegetables ensuring that the cucumbers, carrots and shallot are all about the same size.

Sprinkle about a teaspoon of salt over the chopped vegetables.

Boil water, sugar, salt and vinegar in a pot until the mixture thickens.

Place the red chillies along with the vegetables in a jar and pour the pickling brine over them till the rim to ensure they are well-immersed.

Add water on top, if needed, to cover the vegetables.

Let the pickle cool slightly before storing it in the fridge for at least 48 hours before serving.

Refrigerate until consumed.

22 POMODORI VERDI SOTT'ACETO (ITALIAN TOMATO PICKLE)

One of the world's best-loved foods, be it pizza, pasta, olives, gelato or cheese, Italian cuisine always gets a universal favourite vote. And, of course, we cannot forget the tomatoes, as pizzas and pastas are not complete without Neapolitan sauce. On my trip to Rome, my friend Benny, who is a great chef, invited me to have an authentic Italian meal at his home. I can't forget the stone oven-baked pizzas, which were being freshly baked in his garden. Besides many other dishes, my attention went to the perfect green tomato pickle on the table, of which I must have had a full bowl. The tip he gave me was to use small, unripe, slightly elongated green tomatoes for pickling.

Ingredients

1 kg green tomatoes
100 gm kosher or pink Himalayan salt

1 red bell pepper, sliced
1½ tbsp dried oregano
2 garlic cloves, crushed
1 fresh whole red chilli, chopped
3 sprigs parsley
2½ inch cinnamon sticks (optional)
1½ cups extra virgin olive oil
750 ml white wine vinegar
4–6 black peppercorns

Method

Wash and clean the tomatoes and remove the stems with a knife. Cut them into halves, scoop out the seeds and pulp and slice them.

Rub the salt generously on the tomatoes and leave them overnight in a bowl.

The next day, drain the excess liquid from the tomatoes and wash them under tap water to remove the salt.

Add vinegar and leave them again overnight.

The next day, squeeze the tomatoes and mix them with garlic, oregano, parsley, peppercorns, chillies and sliced and deseeded bell peppers.

Put the marinated tomatoes in a sterilized jar along with the cinnamon and pour olive oil to immerse them fully. If not fully covered, you may add more olive oil on the top.

Seal for 4–5 weeks and after opening, store in the fridge until consumed.

23 SOUTH AMERICAN SOUL GARDEN REFRIGERATOR PICKLE (OKRA OLD-FASHIONED PICKLE)

Crispy, tangy and tasty, pickled okra can be eaten as a snack, used as an accompaniment on your cheeseboard along with pickled onions, olives and cheese, used in your salads and as a garnish or in your hot dogs, burgers, etc.

Okra, although originally from Africa, is very popular in South America, where the okra pickle is immensely popular.

All green vegetables are healthy, and okra is specially rich in minerals, magnesium, calcium, potassium and vitamin A and C.

Here's a classic, easy pickle recipe straight from South America.

Ingredients

1 kg fresh okra (finger-size)
2 cups water

1 tsp dill seeds
2 cups vinegar
3 tbsp kosher salt
2 tbsp red paprika flakes
4 garlic cloves, peeled
1 tsp mustard seeds
1 tsp peppercorns
2 tsp sugar (optional—I use brown sugar)
2 fresh red chilli peppers, slit

Method

Wash okra under running water and trim the stems, leaving the caps intact.

Soak the okra in ice water in a pan for about 1 hour or so.

Drain the water and pat the okra dry.

Clean and sterilize the canning jars.

Alternate the okra heads down and tails down for effective space management in the jar along with the red chilli peppers.

In a non-reactive pan, boil all the pickling ingredients for about 10 minutes and pour over the okra in the jar.

Make sure ½ inch space is left at the top of the jar.

Tap to remove the air bubbles.

Seal the jar tightly with its lid.

Process the jars under a hot water bath for about 10 minutes.

Remove the jars and let them cool to room temperature.

Store the jars in a cool, dry place and let the pickle ferment for about a month.

Once opened, refrigerate it and use within 2 weeks.

24 SOUTH AFRICAN LEMON PICKLE

Lemon is my favourite pickle. I remember my grandmother making some black vintage lemon pickle, which she would always give us when we had stomach aches or indigestion, although I would sometimes blackmail her to let me eat the pickle with my buttered flatbread and cooked lentils. The taste was to die for.

Almost all countries and cultures use preserved lemons as it is one of the most useful medicinal pickles, which aids digestion and, of course, is refreshingly delicious.

South African lemon pickle is versatile and can be eaten with salads and main courses, and can be used as a garnish too.

Ingredients

8 large fresh lemons
¾ cup brown sugar
2 cups apple cider vinegar

2 tsp turmeric powder
1 cup water
1 tbsp mustard seeds
1 red chilli pepper
2 tsp sea salt
1 tsp rock salt

Method

Sterilize the jars.

Cut the lemons into halves and then into thin slices, and remove the pips.

Put the rest of the pickling ingredients, other than red chilli peppers, in a large pan and bring to a boil for about 10 minutes.

Add the lemon slices.

Remove the lemons with a slotted ladle and put in the jars along with chilli peppers.

Pour the brine over it.

Let it cool and tap for air bubbles.

Seal the bottles and let it mature for about 3–4 weeks before use.

25 CEBOLA EM CONSERVA (PORTUGUESE ONION PICKLE)

A popular Portuguese pickle. Onions always make delicious preserves or pickles. I had gone for a summer trip to Portugal and my Portuguese friends carried this pickle to the trek. It goes very well with rye crisps. They told me that this was a non-cumbersome and easy-to-make, no-fuss snack.

Ingredients

10 small white onions
2 large red bell peppers, deseeded and quartered
1 cup water
1 cup wine vinegar
1 tbsp olive oil
1 bay leaf
1 tbsp mustard seeds
1 tbsp dried oregano
2 tsp sugar

1 tsp red chilli flakes
1 tbsp sea salt
2 garlic cloves, crushed
1 tsp caraway seeds

Method

Sterilize some glass jars.

Peel the onions and cut them in quarters or if they are small in size, then use them whole.

Boil the water in a non-reactive pan with vinegar for 5 minutes and mix all the other ingredients together.

Combine onions, garlic and bell peppers in the canning jar.

Pour the hot brine over them.

Ensure that onions, bell peppers and garlic are immersed in the solution.

Leave ½ inch space at the top.

Shake the jar to remove the air bubbles.

Seal the jar and let the pickle rest for one week in the refrigerator before use.

Keep refrigerated after opening until consumed.

26 MAKDOUS (LEBANESE EGGPLANT PICKLE WITH WALNUTS)

Makdous is a part of Middle-Eastern cuisine and it's also popular in Iraq, Jordan, Palestine, Syria and Israel (Levantine cuisine). The Lebanese pickling process is called *mouneh*.

It is made with tiny, tangy aubergines (eggplants) stuffed with spices, walnuts, garlic and olive oil.

This versatile pickle can be used as tapas, in salads, sides and on cheeseboards. I usually mix the makdous with feta cheese and eat it with pita bread or Indian stuffed parantha (flatbread) layered with salad leaves and tomatoes.

Ingredients

6 baby aubergines
3 red bell peppers, coarsely ground
2 tbsp garlic, ground
½ cup walnuts

1 tbsp fresh coriander/parsley, chopped
1½ cups extra virgin olive oil, plus extra if needed
1 tbsp red pepper flakes
2 tbsp pitted olives, chopped
1 tbsp salt

Method

Wash and pat dry the aubergines.

Boil the aubergines for about 12 minutes in water.

Cut the stems.

Drain and set aside until cool.

Make an incision length-wise with a sharp knife without separating it.

Place the aubergines on a flat dish and press with a plate to release excess water.

Maintain the pressure overnight, making sure you drain the dish at night in case the water fills it.

Pound the walnuts, mix in chopped fresh coriander, garlic, red pepper, chopped olives and salt.

Add 50 ml extra virgin olive oil.

Insert the mixture gently in each slit aubergine.

Layer the aubergines in a clean, dry, sterile glass jar.

Add the remaining olive oil ensuring the vegetables are fully covered with oil.

Seal the jar with its lid.

Let it rest for 12–14 days in a dark place and store at room temperature.

The pickle will be good for about 12 months if well covered with olive oil.

27 ISRAELI PICKLED TURNIPS

Pickled turnips are the pickle of the Middle East, abundantly eaten with shawarmas, falafel, lamb or chicken roast, and they are completely addictive. The luscious pink pickle is vinegary and fiery.

I love to eat it with falafel stuffed with feta, olives or in pita bread with hummus or sour cream sizzle.

The pickle can be used as a garnish, accompaniment or side dish as per your choice.

Ingredients

3 cups water
1 tsp sugar
⅓ cup kosher salt
1 cup white vinegar
1 kg turnips, peeled
1 large beet, sliced
2 garlic cloves

1 tbsp red pepper powder
2 bay leaves
6 pink peppercorns

Method

In a pan, boil water with bay leaves, sugar, vinegar and salt for about 10 minutes. Remove from the fire and let it cool to room temperature.

Add red pepper powder.

In sterilized jars, put peeled turnips—cut in strips or quarters as you prefer—garlic, peppercorns and sliced beets.

Pour in the hot brine solution, immersing all the vegetables.

Remove the bubbles by tapping the jar.

Seal the jar with its lid.

Store for 1 week in a cool, dark place.

Refrigerate and store for a month.

28 AGLIO MARINATO
(ITALIAN MARINATED GARLIC PICKLE)

Garlic is one of most popular ingredients in Italian cooking. From pasta to pizza or even pickle, Italians liberally use garlic in their food.

Marinated garlic can be used while cooking or even as an aperitif on a slice of bread or lavash.

You will always find this garlic pickle on my cheeseboard. Just add it to your cheese and crackers, and you will love it. I even use it extensively in my pastas, sandwiches and bakes.

Ingredients

4 heads of fresh garlic, cloves separated
1 tsp sea salt
1 red bell pepper, cut in small pieces
1 tsp black pepper, coarsely crushed
1 bay leaf
½ tsp red chilli flakes

1 tsp dried oregano
4 cloves
2 cups distilled white vinegar
⅓ cup extra virgin olive oil

Method

Clean the garlic, separate the heads and peel the outer skin.

In a non-reactive saucepan, pour the vinegar, add salt, chilli flakes, cloves, pepper, oregano and bay leaf, and bring the solution to a boil for about 10 minutes. Remove from heat and bring the pickling brine to room temperature.

Mix in the olive oil.

Prepare a sterilized glass jar for pickling.

Put the garlic and bell pepper in the sterilized jar and top up with the brine.

Leave ½ inch space at the top and shake the jar to remove all the air bubbles.

Seal the jar with the lid.

Store for about a month in a dry and dark place before use.

After opening, refrigerate it until consumed.

29 MUKHALAL (LEBANESE SHAWARMA PICKLE)

We all fancy shawarma rolls, laden with pickles, sour cream, falafel and hummus. It is one of the most tasty and globally popular dishes. It can be eaten as a snack or main course. The shawarma pickle made with pink turnip, cucumber, beets, etc., in vinegar provides a crunchy punch to the rolls.

So, let's see how to make this tasty pickle. I usually store it and have it in burgers, sandwiches and as an accompaniment on my cheeseboard too.

Ingredients

1 large cucumber, seeds removed and cut into sticks
1 large carrot, peeled and cut into sticks
1 small beet, cut into sticks
1 turnip, julienned
2–3 big green chillies
4–6 garlic cloves

1 tsp mustard seeds
¼ tsp coriander seeds
150 ml red wine vinegar or white distilled vinegar as per taste
300 ml boiled water, at room temperature
1 tsp kosher salt
2 tbsp brown sugar

Method

Put all vegetables, except cucumber, in a saucepan.

Cover with a lid and parboil them for 2 minutes.

Boil all the brine solution ingredients with all the spices and condiments.

Sterilize and clean a jar.

Put the vegetables and cucumbers in the jar, pour in the hot pickling solution leaving ½ inch space at the top and seal with the lid.

Let it rest for 24 hours and then store in the fridge until consumed.

30 TURSU
(TURKISH VEGETABLE PICKLE)

All across the Middle East, the mixed vegetable or single vegetable pickles are enjoyed with salads, main courses, sandwiches, falafel, etc.

This recipe is simple and one can make it with one or different vegetables as per your choice—the process will remain the same. You may choose all those vegetables you would like to store and eat.

Ingredients

2 large carrots
4 jalapeño chillies
2 cucumbers
2 turnips
1 tbsp parsley, chopped
½ cup white distilled vinegar
1½ cups water

2 tbsp rock salt
1 tbsp brown sugar
10 black peppercorns
½ tsp grated ginger
2 tsp sesame seeds, roasted (optional)

Method

Cut the vegetables in sticks and slice the turnips.

In a non-reactive pan, boil the water and vinegar.

Add spices and sugar along with ginger and boil for 10 minutes.

Prepare a canning jar, sterilize it and clean-dry it.

Add the vegetables (jalapeños, chopped parsley and turnips at the end) in the jar and sprinkle sesame seeds (if using them) on top.

Pour the hot pickling solution over the vegetables.

Let the vegetables rest for about 30 minutes.

Seal the jar tightly with the lid and refrigerate for about 24 hours before use.

31 KABEES EL LIFT PICKLE (LEBANESE FERMENTED PICKLED TURNIPS)

You must have noticed decorated vegetables, olives and pickles in large glass jars along the windows or displayed on the sideboards of classic Arabian restaurants. I am always fascinated on seeing such beautiful, colourful pickled vegetables, large green chillies, fruits, etc., in the windows of these restaurants when I'm visiting the Middle East.

Lebanese fermented pickled turnips, with their beautiful dark pink colour, enhance the flavour of meze, shawarma, meats and pita sandwiches, and can be used as garnishes as well.

With all my research in pickling, distilled vinegar works better with turnips than apple cider vinegar.

Ingredients

5 medium turnips
2 small ripe beetroots

3 cups distilled vinegar
3½ cups water
¼ cup garlic, chopped
8 tbsp kosher salt
2 bay leaves
5 peppercorns (optional)
2 whole red chilli peppers

Method

Sterilize your jars, and clean-dry them.

Peel the turnips and slice them in thick discs.

Peel the beets and slice them in discs.

In a non-reactive pan, heat vinegar and water with all the condiments and seasoning.

Bring it to a boil and simmer for about 10 minutes.

Let it cool to room temperature.

Put the beets and turnips in the jar alternatively.

Pour the hot pickling solution along with the condiments into the jar.

Keep ½ inch space at the top and don't fill the solution till the rim.

Tap the jar to remove any air bubbles.

Close the lid tightly and let the pickle rest at room temperature for about 6 days.

Store in the refrigerator.

32 TURSHI LEFT (PERSIAN TURNIP PICKLE)

Pickled turnips are called 'turshi left', in which beets are added to impart a bright pink colour.

They are part of most Arabian mezes and can accompany mains. They are also used in falafels, wraps and salads, and can be used as garnishes too.

Ingredients

1 kg turnips
1 medium ripe beetroot
6 garlic cloves, crushed
½ tsp red chilli flakes
2 stalks of celery, sliced

Brine

2½ cups water

1½ cups white vinegar
2 tbsp kosher salt
1 tbsp olive oil

Method

Sterilize your jars and dry them.

Wash and clean turnips, celery and beet.

Peel them and cut turnips in juliennes or in quarters as you prefer.

Peel and cut beet in round diskettes.

Rub chilli flakes on the vegetables and add garlic cloves.

Put turnips, beet and celery in the jar.

In a pan, bring water, vinegar and salt to a boil for about 10 minutes and add olive oil.

Pour the hot pickling brine over the turnips, celery and beet.

Ensure that there is ½ inch space at the top.

Top up with olive oil if required.

Tap to remove air bubbles and seal with the lid.

Store in a cool place for 12 days and let it ferment.

After opening, refrigerate—the pickle can be used for a month.

33 OGORKI KISZONE (POLISH BRINE-CURED CUKES/ SOUR CUCUMBER PICKLE)

In Poland, pickles are made with vinegar and their favourite small sour cucumbers are preserved in brine. Preserved cucumbers are refreshing with the addition of cherry or raspberry leaves, which help in the fermentation process. Leaves that contain tannin help in lacto-fermentation and keep the cucumbers crisp and sour.

I love eating preserved cucumbers with my salads, mezes and sandwiches.

Ingredients

12 6-inch-long pickling cucumbers
2 cups distilled white vinegar
2 tbsp sea salt
1 litre filtered water
2 tbsp mustard seeds

3 garlic cloves
1 dill stem with seeds
2 bay leaves
1 1-inch piece fresh horseradish root
3–4 pink peppercorns
3–4 cherry leaves

Method

Wash and clean the cucumbers.

Tightly squeeze the cucumbers in a sterilized jar.

In a non-reactive pan, bring water, vinegar and salt to a boil and let it simmer for about 10 minutes.

Add all the other ingredients—peppercorns, bay leaves, horseradish root, mustard seeds, garlic, cherry leaves and dill—in the pickling brine and pour over the cucumbers in the jar leaving ½ inch space at the top.

Tap to release any air bubbles.

Seal the jar.

Store in a cool place for about 5 weeks for fermentation.

Refrigerate after opening until consumed.

34 DANISH WHITE CUCUMBER PICKLE

This recipe was given to me by a friend's mother. She would make these incredible Danish open-face chicken sandwiches with these delightful and tasty pickled cucumbers.

This is a lovely, white, crisp and sweet pickle that can accompany almost everything, from snacks to starters, mains, salads, etc. *Asier* (meaning 'beginning') refers to a type of cucumber served traditionally in Denmark along with roast pork and braised red cabbage.

I love cucumbers and pickling makes them even tastier. Cucumbers are healthy as well as low in calories and contain 90 per cent water, making them a good source for hydration in summer months. Cucumbers are rich in vitamin K, and have traces of minerals like copper, phosphorus and manganese.

Since cucumber peel has good nutritional value, one can pickle them with the peels, although the traditional recipe is without the peel.

Ingredients

6 medium stiff cucumbers, unwaxed
½ cup apple cider vinegar
½ cup water
2½ tbsp sugar or stevia as per taste
1 tbsp sea salt
2 tbsp fresh dill
½ tsp white pepper
2 whole red chilli peppers
2 tbsp fresh chopped parsley

Method

Wash, dry and peel the cucumbers and then slice them thinly. You may use unpeeled cucumbers too.

In a bowl, add water, vinegar, salt, pepper and sugar, and boil for 10 minutes.

In a jar, tightly pack the cucumbers and dill.

Add the red chilli peppers and pour the hot pickling brine over them.

Tap the jar for air bubbles to escape and then cover the lid tightly.

Refrigerate for at least 3 hours before use.

Serve after draining and sprinkle fresh parsley as garnish.

35 TOURSI
(TRADITIONAL GREEK
ASSORTED VEGETABLE PICKLE)

Greeks love pickled vegetables and use them as a side dish, accompaniments with mains, in salads, burgers and sandwiches. *Toursi* is the Greek word for pickles. It is a common traditional way to preserve vegetables during winter months. Some vegetables normally used to make toursi are cauliflower, string beans, red bell peppers, green chilli peppers and carrots, which are combined with brine or vinegar solution. Every region in the world has its own unique way of making vegetable pickles.

Ingredients

1 large white onion
1 medium broccoli
2 medium turnips
1 medium cauliflower

1 celery stem
4 medium orange carrots
4 medium stiff cucumbers
4 red bell peppers
6 long spicy green peppers
4 garlic cloves
1–2 bay leaves
8 pink peppercorns
6–7 cherry or raspberry leaves
1 tbsp fennel seeds
1 litre wine vinegar
1 litre water
1 cup olive oil
3 tbsp sea salt
100 gm sugar
5–6 ½ litre jars that can be well-sealed

Method

Rinse the vegetables well.

Peel the carrots and cut them into sticks.

Cut the cauliflower and broccoli into small florets.

Cut the turnips into small cubes.

Slice the rest of the vegetables, other than green chilli peppers, which will be used whole.

Place all of the vegetables in a basin with the salt and leave overnight to drain excess moisture.

In a non-reactive pan, heat water and vinegar with sugar and salt for about 10 minutes.

Add peppercorns, garlic, onions, fennel seeds, bay leaves and cherry or raspberry leaves in the sterilized jars.

Put the assorted vegetables in the jars except green peppers, which will be placed on the top.

Fill the jars with hot pickling brine ensuring all the vegetables are covered and then top it up with olive oil.

Seal the jars tightly; remember to tap to release the air bubbles before sealing.

Do the canning process as described earlier.

Cool the jars to room temperature.

Store in a cool place and use after 24 hours.

Once opened, refrigerate until consumed.

36 LATIN BIRD PEPPER PICKLE

Bird peppers are tiny hot peppers that grow during summer months in Latin America. We all know the best way to preserve food is to pickle it and enjoy it during the season when it is not available.

I love pepper pickles, being a true Punjabi, and I have always indulged in the red stuffed long chilli peppers. I remember my grandmother making it specially for the family, which we enjoyed eating with aloo paranthas (fried potato pancakes) and artisan white butter.

On my trip to Rio, I found this incredible pepper pickle and fell in love with it, besides other things, obviously. In Mexico, these peppers are called chiles de monte or more popularly, chile piquin. The pickle takes about 15 minutes to make and the ingredients are commonly available in most kitchens.

So, let's try this incredibly simple recipe.

Ingredients

1 kg bird peppers
1 small red carrot, thinly sliced
4 garlic cloves
5 peppercorns
½ tsp cumin seeds
¼ white onion, thinly sliced
1 tsp Mexican oregano
2 bay leaves
2 small fresh thyme sprigs
1 cup distilled white vinegar
2 tbsp extra virgin olive oil
1 tsp sea salt

Method

In a pan, heat vinegar with bay leaves, peppercorns, cumin and salt and bring to a boil. Simmer for about 10 minutes.

Put the peppers along with other vegetables in sterilized jars.

Add Mexican oregano and thyme.

Pour the hot pickling brine mixture over this and add olive oil on top.

Remember to leave an inch of space at the top and tap to remove air bubbles.

Seal the jars tightly and give them a warm water bath.

Keep in a cool, dark place for 5 days before use.

Once opened, refrigerate until consumed.

37 PERU CHE LONCHE (GUAVA PICKLE)

This is an Indian pickle, popular in Maharashtra. In Marathi, *peru* means 'guava' and *lonche* means 'pickle'.

I discovered this amazing pickle in 2008 when we opened our first Moti Mahal outlet in Mumbai. One of our Marathi chefs made it for me to sample for one of our food festivals. Although this easy-to-make fruity pickle has a shorter shelf life, it is worth making in small quantities again and again in season. Serve along with rice and curry—it's delicious.

Ingredients

500 gm guava
250 gm jaggery
2 tbsp imli/tamarind paste
⅓ tsp methi seeds (fenugreek seeds)
1 tsp red chilli powder
½ tsp turmeric powder

½ tsp asafoetida
1 tsp sesame seeds, roasted
4–6 pink peppercorns
2 tsp salt
1 tbsp oil
½ cup water

Method

Cut the guava and scoop out the seeds.

Cut the seedless guava into small cubes.

Heat oil in a pan, on medium heat.

Add fenugreek seeds, sesame seeds, peppercorns and asafoetida.

Add guava pieces and sauté.

Add red chilli powder, turmeric powder and salt. Mix well.

Mix in jaggery and tamarind paste.

Add water, cover for 3–4 minutes and let it simmer on low heat.

Remove the lid, give the pickle one more boil and turn off the heat.

Bring to room temperature and store in the refrigerator. It remains fresh for 3–4 days.

Enjoy with paranthas or pita bread, or rice and curry.

38 COLOMBIAN VEGETABLE PICKLE

Colombia is one of the biggest megadiverse countries; its territory encompasses the Amazon rainforest, highlands, grasslands and deserts. Colombia's cuisine is influenced by its diverse fauna and flora as well as the cultural traditions of its ethnic groups. Colombian dishes vary widely by region. Some of the most common ingredients are cereals, such as rice and maize, tubers, such as potato, fruits, fruit juices, vegetables, meats and poultry. Colombians make a wide variety of colourful vegetable pickles, which they consume as relishes, side dishes and in salads.

Ingredients

½ cup red bell peppers
1 bunch dill leaves with seeds
½ cup stiff cucumber slices
¼ cup cauliflower, cut into small florets
½ cup broccoli, cut into small florets

¼ cup carrots, diced
2 whole red chilli peppers
½ cup white vinegar
1 tbsp kosher salt
5 garlic cloves
½ tsp mustard seeds or celery seeds
1 tsp red pepper flakes
2 cups water
1 tbsp honey
1 litre Mason jar with lid

Method

Heat the vinegar, salt and honey in a saucepan with 2 cups of water and bring to a boil.

Stir until salt and honey are dissolved.

Sterilize and clean the jar.

Place red pepper flakes, mustard or celery seeds and garlic in the jar.

Add the vegetables and place the dill leaves with seeds on the top.

Pour in the boiling pickling mixture.

Ensure that there is 1 inch space at the top.

Tap to remove the air bubbles and seal the jar with the lid.

Store in a cool place for minimum 24 hours.

Place in the refrigerator after use. The pickle remains fresh for about a week.

39 MALAY ACHCHARU (SRI LANKAN MALAY PICKLE)

Malay achcharu is widely used in Sri Lanka and often accompanies their much-loved biryani. Traditionally, it was made with pineapple and mangoes, but Malays also prefer assorted vegetable pickle. It is sweet and tangy, and flavoured with pitted dates.

It's a healthy, colourful, fermented relish with a powerful, distinctive taste that enhances the flavours of the main dish. On a trip to hold a food festival in our Moti Mahal restaurant in Colombo, this pickle was a part of our menu along with a few Indo–Sri Lankan dishes and Indian snacks like stuffed samosa and pickled kachori.

Ingredients

2 carrots, cut in small sticks
1 red bell pepper, sliced
1 green bell pepper, sliced

½ cup green beans, cut in 1-inch length
2 red onions, peeled and sliced
4 garlic cloves
4 large green hot peppers
2 tbsp red chilli flakes
1 tbsp plus 1 cup kosher salt
1 1-inch ginger piece, peeled
1 cup pitted dates
1 tbsp granulated brown sugar
2 tsp mustard seeds
½ cup plus 2 tbsp white vinegar

Method

Clean the vegetables and rub salt over them.

Spread over a cloth and keep overnight to drain excess water.

In a food processor, blend pitted dates, sugar, red chilli flakes, 2 tbsp vinegar and salt into a thick paste.

In a non-reactive pan, heat vinegar and the paste for a few minutes.

Place all the vegetables in a sterilized jar, along with mustard seeds and ginger.

Pour the hot brine over them, covering all the vegetables.

Seal the lid tightly and store in a cool, dark place for 5 days for fermentation.

Refrigerate for about 2 weeks before use.

40 MALDIVIAN FISH PICKLE

Maldivians love their tuna, which I discovered when I opened my restaurant Moti Mahal in the Maldives, a few years ago. The corporate chef who hailed from the Maldives insisted that we add a few dishes made with tuna. He went to the extent of making butter tuna as a tribute to our butter chicken, which was invented by my grandfather, Kundan Lal Gujral.

The Maldivians eat tuna for breakfast, tuna for lunch and, of course, tuna for dinner. So, here we go with tuna preserve—a delicious recipe for you all!

Ingredients

1 kg tuna
2 tbsp ginger, chopped
2 tbsp garlic, chopped
Vegetable oil to fry the fish
⅓ cup coconut oil
8 green chillies, slit

6 curry leaves
2 tsp granulated sugar (you can even add raw honey or jaggery)
1 tbsp red chilli powder
½ tsp turmeric powder
½ tsp black pepper powder
1 tsp mustard seeds
1 tsp roasted fenugreek powder
1 tsp asafoetida powder
2 tsp tamarind water
1 cup vinegar

Marinade

2 tbsp red chilli powder
1 tbsp black pepper powder
1 tsp turmeric powder
1 tbsp salt

Method

Clean and cut tuna into small chunks or cubes and marinate with red chilli, turmeric powder, black pepper and salt.

Keep aside for 30 minutes.

Fry tuna pieces in oil and keep aside.

Heat oil in a pan, add mustard seeds and cook until they splutter.

Add curry leaves, green chillies and chopped ginger and garlic. Sauté for 2–3 minutes.

Add red chilli powder, turmeric powder, sugar/honey/jaggery (as per your choice), salt and pepper, and sauté again for 2–3 minutes.

Add tamarind water and vinegar and let it boil.

Add fried tuna and cook for 2 minutes.

Add asafoetida powder and fenugreek powder and turn off the heat.

Store in clean, sterilized glass jars.

Top up with more coconut oil if needed as it helps to preserve the fish pickle.

Store in a cool, dry place.

41 PICKLED ARMENIAN CUCUMBERS AND GHERKINS

It is a simple pickle used in burgers, mezes and sandwiches, as relishes, etc. One can make a few jars in just a few minutes. The flavouring in cucumber pickle is enhanced by dill seeds and blackcurrant leaves. Persian or Kirby cucumbers are commonly used for making the pickle as they have thin skin and remain crisp for a long time. It's a versatile pickle that can complement most dishes and can even be eaten as a snack.

Ingredients

½ kg stiff medium cucumbers, sliced ¼ inch thick
½ kg gherkins
2 stalks celery
¼ cup dill leaves
¾ cup dill flower heads, coarsely chopped
½ tsp dill seeds
1 tsp red chilli flakes

½ tsp peppercorns
1½ tsp mustard seeds
1 tsp coriander seeds
4 garlic cloves, chopped
2 tbsp brown sugar
2 whole red chillies to add some spice
2 cups hot water
2 cups white vinegar
3 tbsp sea salt or kosher salt
2–3 cherry or blackcurrant leaves to infuse some aroma

Method

In a non-reactive pan, combine vinegar, water, sugar, salt, mustard seeds, coriander seeds, red chilli flakes, peppercorns and dill seeds and bring to a boil for 10 minutes.

Remove from heat and cool.

Sterilize the pickling jars.

Make tiny holes in the cucumbers and gherkins with a toothpick so they can absorb the brine.

Place the pickling cucumbers, gherkins and celery stalks in the jars and add dill leaves, dill heads, blackcurrant or cherry leaves and chopped garlic.

Pour the brine solution over the pickles ensuring ½ inch space on the top and tap to remove air bubbles before sealing the jar.

Refrigerate the pickles overnight, occasionally shaking the jars.

Serve cold and refrigerate until consumed.

42 TURKISH VEGETABLE PICKLE

Pickles are very important in Turkish cuisine. One can see a sea of shops in the markets displaying the most colourful varieties of pickles, cured in brine or vinegar. I learnt from one of my friends, who runs a successful restaurant in Istanbul, that the ideal pickling solution should have equal parts water and vinegar and, of course, some sea salt. He told me never to use table salt for making pickles.

Although there are many variations of tursu or vegetable and fruit pickles in Turkey, as almost every region has its own recipe, I found this fruit and vegetable pickle recipe very unique and so, I am sharing it with you.

Ingredients

2 cups green bell peppers
2 cups cabbage, chopped
½ cup jalapeño peppers
2 cups carrots

2 cups gherkins
1 cup pickling onions
4 garlic cloves
½ cup Cornelian cherries
1 large beetroot
2 tbsp vine leaves
250 ml distilled white vinegar
4 cups water
2 tbsp sea salt
1 tbsp brown sugar or raw honey
10 black peppercorns
1 1-inch piece ginger

Method

Cut and clean the vegetables.

Chop green peppers in roundels, and wash and clean the cherries.

In a non-reactive pan, add water, black peppercorns, ginger, sugar or honey and salt, and heat on medium.

Add vinegar and allow it to cool to room temperature.

In a sterilized jar, put some garlic cloves and cherries, and cover with vine leaves.

Thereafter, add some vegetables.

Pour the pickling brine over the vegetables.

Repeat the layers until the jar is full till 1 inch below the rim.

Let it sit overnight. Refrigerate and start using.

43 HUNGARIAN PEPPER PICKLE

Hungarian hot peppers have a moderate amount of heat, which is usually measured in units called Scoville units. Hungarian peppers have 5000–10,000 Scoville units as compared to hot tabasco peppers, which have 30,000–70,000 Scoville units. These are used fresh in salsas, dips, mezes, platters and salads, pickled or in relishes, and as an ingredient in stews, soups and marinades. They can be grilled with other barbeque dishes.

I love to eat the Hungarian pickled peppers in hot dogs with melted cheese and sausages.

Ingredients

2 cups white vinegar
1 cup water
6 garlic cloves
2 cinnamon sticks, ½ inch long
1 tsp mustard seeds

½ tsp pink peppercorns
2 bay leaves
2 tbsp sugar/raw honey
2 tsp coarse sea salt
12–15 hot peppers, washed and dried, seeded and cut into strips

Method

In a non-reactive saucepan, heat white vinegar and 1 cup water. Bring it to a boil and simmer for 10 minutes. Remove from heat and keep aside.

Sterilize the jars, divide the ingredients equally as per the number of jars.

Put garlic cloves, bay leaves, cinnamon sticks, mustard seeds, pickling salt, sugar/honey, pink peppercorns and hot peppers in the jar, leaving 1 inch head space.

Pour in the hot pickling brine to cover the peppers.

Shake the jar to remove any air bubbles and seal it tightly.

Follow the hot water bath canning process and store in a cool, dark place for 48 hours before consuming. Keep refrigerated until consumed.

44 PANAMANIAN FRIED PICKLES

The first time I heard about fried pickles, I was amazed as I had never eaten any fried pickle before. However, when I discovered the recipe, it reminded me of our pakoras or fritters; the only difference is that we use raw vegetables, cottage cheese and chicken normally. In Panama, they use pickled dill or any refrigerator pickles instead and dip it with ranch dressing while eating it as a snack.

Ingredients

½ cup vegetable oil for frying
½ tsp cayenne pepper
¼ tsp Italian seasoning
½ tsp garlic powder
½ tsp black pepper
1 tbsp hot sauce
½ cup all-purpose flour
1 tsp sea salt

2 cups pickled dill
½ cup water

Method

Heat oil in a heavy-bottomed pot over medium-high heat.

In a shallow bowl, whisk together flour, Italian seasoning, garlic powder, salt and pepper.

Add hot sauce and water, and mix until a smooth batter is formed.

Add pickled dill to the batter in batches and gently toss to coat.

Using a slotted spoon, remove coated pickles from the batter and let the excess drip off.

Fry pickles in the oil until golden.

Remove and let drain on paper towels.

Serve hot with ranch dressing.

45 TASMANIAN PICKLED ONIONS

Tasmanian pickled onions can be enjoyed as a snack or with meals. Garnish the top of your favourite dish with this super crunchy and tangy, delightful pickle. I had gone to Australia for a gourmet tour, where I met Tim, who was on the same tour, visiting from Tasmania. We all had to demonstrate one of our favourite easy-to-make recipes as part of the programme. Tim made a delicious pita sandwich with mayo, olives, sundried tomatoes and Tasmanian pickled onions, chopped and mixed with tuna salad. It was one of the best sandwiches I had ever tasted.

So, you may want to try making a tuna salad sandwich with this pickle at home too.

Ingredients

4 cups water
⅓ cup salt
1 kg pickling onions, sliced

3 cups cider or white vinegar
4–5 cloves
4–5 pink peppercorns
1 1-inch cinnamon stick
3 cardamom pods
2 bay leaves
1¾ tsp all-spice powder (recipe on page 6)
½ tbsp brown sugar
1 small beet, chopped

Method

Heat water and salt and allow to cool.

Add onion slices and chopped beet.

Let it rest overnight.

Combine the vinegar with spices, peppercorns and sugar.

In a sterilized jar, add onions drained from the salty brine.

Pour the vinegar-spice mix over the onions and seal the lid.

Let it rest for a few days until the fermentation is as per your taste.

Then store in the fridge until consumed.

46 DUTCH PICKLED EGGS AND BEET

Whenever I visit the Netherlands, I have to try the Dutch egg pickle. I know a special place in a nondescript area where this old lady makes sandwiches with pickled eggs and coleslaw. It's to die for with a cup of espresso followed by Dutch chocolate cake. Hmmmm!

Ingredients

6 hard-boiled eggs, peeled
1 onion, thinly sliced
400 gm canned pickled beets
1½ cups white vinegar
1 cup sugar
¾ cup cider
1 tsp salt
½ tsp black pepper
1 bay leaf

8 cloves, whole
1 1-inch cinnamon stick

Method

Remove the beets from the can and reserve the juice.

In a bowl, place the beets, onions and eggs.

In a separate pan, add the reserved juice, white vinegar, sugar, cloves, bay leaf, salt, pepper and cinnamon and bring to a boil.

Reduce the heat and let it simmer for 12–15 minutes.

Pour the pickling brine over the beets, eggs and onion slices.

Seal the jar and refrigerate for 3 days before serving.

Keep refrigerated until consumed.

47 PHILIPPINE KODUKAPULI (PICKLED TAMARIND)

It's a popular pickle in the Philippines, used as an accompaniment to the main course and salads.

Ingredients

1½ cups sweet tamarind pulp
½ tsp turmeric powder
3 curry leaves, crushed
1 tsp kosher salt
1 tsp chilli powder
1 tsp mustard seeds
½ tsp asafoetida
¼ tsp fenugreek seeds
4 red chillies, cut in roundels
1 tbsp jaggery
4 tbsp mustard oil
8 garlic cloves

Method

Heat oil in a wok.

Add garlic, cook until it is light brown.

Add mustard seeds and fenugreek seeds; cook until they splutter.

Add crushed curry leaves, asafoetida and chilli roundels.

Mix in jaggery and tamarind pulp, and cook until it is fully mixed.

Add salt, turmeric and chilli powder.

Sauté for about 2 minutes and remove from heat.

Allow it to cool to room temperature.

Store in an airtight container and refrigerate for use.

48 RUSSIAN PICKLED TOMATOES

Russia has severe winters. They too preserve their food by fermenting or pickling it. Tomatoes are one of the most versatile vegetables, which can be pickled or used in salads or cooking. This particular pickle, popular in Russia, can be served with soups, as a side dish and also in meze.

1 kg ripe cherry or plum tomatoes
4 garlic cloves, sliced
1 stalk green onion, chopped with root end discarded
2 tbsp whole black peppercorns
6 tbsp sea salt
2 tbsp brown sugar
2 tbsp distilled white wine vinegar
2 tsp dill seeds, crushed
3 oak, blackcurrant or cherry leaves
1 bunch fresh parsley
1 bunch tarragon leaves

1 small bunch dill with dill flowers
4 bay leaves
3–4 sprigs fresh thyme
1 6-inch piece horseradish, peeled and sliced

Method

Take 4 litres water in a non-reactive jar and add peppercorns, salt, vinegar and sugar.

Boil for 10 minutes.

Sterilize and clean the jars.

Put tomatoes, garlic, bay leaves, parsley, dill, dill seeds, green onions, oak or cherry leaves, tarragon leaves, thyme and horseradish in the jars in such a way that they surround the tomatoes.

Pour the hot pickling brine over the tomatoes saving 1 inch space at the top.

Shake to remove the bubbles, if any, and seal the jar tightly with its lid.

Give the jars a canning bath, then place them upside down for around 3 days.

Refrigerate once opened. It can be used up to 1 month post opening the jars.

49 RUSSIAN PICKLED CUCUMBERS

Cucumber, being a summer vegetable, is preserved by the Russians by pickling, due to its non-availability in cold winter months.

I remember my grandfather travelled to Russia in the 1960s when it was a closed country. Premier Nikita Khrushchev was so impressed by our butter chicken and tandoori kebabs that he invited my grandfather to set up Moti Mahal for one month in Moscow. On his return, besides many toys and decorative items, my grandfather had brought along food items too, for us to taste. I clearly remember a small cucumber pickle jar among those items. Sometimes, childhood memories can bring up something special.

Ingredients

1 kg stiff pickling cucumbers
2 cups water
1 cup white wine vinegar

1 tbsp sea salt
1 tsp granulated sugar
4 garlic cloves, peeled and sliced
6 dill stalks with flowers
1 tsp peppercorns
6 tarragon leaves
8 blackcurrant leaves
3 sprigs fresh thyme
1 1-inch horseradish piece, peeled and sliced

Method

Sterilize glass Mason jars and clean-dry them.

Prepare the pickling brine by boiling water, vinegar, salt, sugar and peppercorns for about 10 minutes.

Wash and pat dry the cucumbers, and cut them length-wise into 4 spears.

In the Mason jars, add half of the garlic, horseradish, dill, tarragon leaves, blackcurrant leaves and thyme, then add cucumbers.

Thereafter, add the remaining half of the garlic, thyme, horseradish, tarragon leaves, blackcurrant leaves and dill.

Pour the hot pickling solution over the cucumbers and seal the jar with cheesecloth.

Let it rest for 2 days for the fermentation.

When the brine becomes cloudy, refrigerate and use within 1 week.

50 THAI PICKLED RADISH

A peculiar yet delicious pickle from Thailand. Radishes are not only peppery and crunchy but also a great source of vitamin C, fibre, riboflavin and potassium. Radishes are also good as pickles and can be fermented into fiery kimchi.

Pickled radishes can be paired with tacos, burgers, noodles, soup and salads.

Ingredients

12 radishes (white and red)
1½ tbsp salt
3–4 garlic cloves
2 whole red chilli peppers
2 cups water
3 tbsp soy sauce
6 tbsp rice wine vinegar
2 tbsp honey
2 tsp toasted sesame seeds

Method

Peel and finely chop the garlic cloves.

Rinse the radishes, peel them and cut into discs.

Mix honey, rice vinegar, water, soy sauce, salt and garlic, and boil in a non-reactive pan.

In sterilized glass jars, put the radish and red chilli peppers.

Sprinkle the toasted sesame seeds and pour the hot pickling brine over the radish.

Seal tightly.

Store for 2–3 days until fermented to your taste and refrigerate for use.

51 BASAL TAL PICKLES (MALTA'S PICKLED ONIONS)

Malta is a tourist destination with a warm climate, numerous recreational areas and architectural and historical monuments, including three UNESCO World Heritage Sites. It's part of the European Union and so we find a predominance of European cuisine here.

During the launch of my book, *On the Dessert Trail*, at a hotel in Delhi, the head pastry chef was from Malta. From him, I learnt many Maltese desserts and got this onion pickle recipe too. He told me that one of the positive aspects of pickled onions is that they do not leave a foul smell in your mouth after eating them, so one can eat them whenever one feels like it; in meals or salads or as a snack with crackers and cheese.

Ingredients

500 shallots/white medium onions

2–3 cherry leaves
1½ cups malt vinegar
3 tsp Worcestershire sauce
3 dried bay leaves
2 tsp salt
1 tsp pink peppercorns
2 large red bell peppers, sliced
2 tbsp granulated sugar (brown sugar—optional)
5 garlic cloves, peeled
2 fresh rosemary sprigs
Extra virgin olive oil to top up

Method

In a pan, put the vinegar, Worcestershire sauce, bay leaves, rosemary, sugar, salt and peppercorns, and bring to a boil.

Lower the heat and let it simmer for 5–6 minutes.

Peel the shallots/onions by removing the first and second layers of the outer skin and cut the top and the base.

Place them in a sterilized jar along with the cherry leaves and garlic, and top it with the prepared brine along with all the condiments that were boiled in it.

Close the lid and give the jar a shake so the brine and onions settle.

Open the lid and top up with olive oil to keep the air out.

Place a piece of butter paper on the rim and close the lid.

Keep in the sun for 2–3 weeks and keep shaking occasionally.

Store in a cool place.

52 CALIFORNIAN QUICK ORANGE PICKLE

The moment you think about California, you visualize large, juicy Californian oranges. Orange juice, orange desserts and orange salads all taste great in California, somehow.

We last visited California on our twentieth wedding anniversary, and I remember having this pickle at breakfast in a hotel by the sea.

The chef was kind enough to give me this recipe, of course, in exchange for a few Indian recipes that he made with me later in the kitchen to learn them better.

Ingredients

8 fresh Californian oranges
1½ tsp fresh lemon juice
1 tsp brown sugar
½ tsp all-spice powder (recipe on page 6)
4 fresh large green chilli peppers, chopped
1 tsp cayenne pepper

½ tsp asafoetida
1 tsp black salt
5 tsp extra virgin olive oil

Method

Peel the oranges, separate the segments and chop them into three pieces.

Remove the seeds.

In a bowl, mix all the spices, chopped chilli peppers, lemon juice and oil.

Keep covered for 15–20 minutes to soak in the flavours.

Refrigerate until consumed. Serve chilled.

53 ACHARI ANGOOR (INDIAN GRAPE PICKLE)

Grapes are my favourite fruit, not because I love wine as you may have thought, but because it's a very versatile fruit. Dry them and you get raisins, squash them and you get wine, eat them raw as a fruit or use them in salads or curries—they taste divine.

Let's make this simple but mouth-watering Indian grape pickle.

Ingredients

2½ cups seedless grapes (green and black mix)
1 whole red chilli
1 tsp red chilli powder
¼ tsp black salt
2½ tsp all-spice powder (recipe on page 6)
1 tsp sea salt
¼ tsp asafoetida

1½ tsp lemon juice
½ tsp granulated sugar
4 tsp olive oil

Method

Wash grapes, wipe them dry and put them in a bowl.

Add all the spices, lemon juice, red chilli pepper and oil, and mix well.

Keep covered for 2 hours and then fill it in a glass jar.

Keep refrigerated for a week.

Giardiniera
(Italian Pickled Vegetables)

L'hamd Markad
(Moroccan Preserved Lemons)

Kyuri Asa-Zuke
(Japanese Pickled Cucumbers)

Torshi Left
(Israeli Turnip Pickle)

Kimchi
(South Korean Vegetable Pickle)

German Sauerkraut

Gari
(Japanese Ginger Pickle)

Inlagda Rödbetor
(Scandinavian Beet Pickle)

The UK's Pickled Eggs

Tsukemono
(Japanese Mixed Vegetable Pickle)

Pikliz
(Haitian Pickled Relish)

Jalapeños en Escabeche
(Mexican Pickled Jalapeño Peppers)

Sirka Pyaaz
(Indian Vinegar Onions)

Makdous
(Lebanese Eggplant Pickle with Walnuts)

Aglio Marinato
(Italian Marinated Garlic Pickle)

Mukhalal
(Lebanese Shawarma Pickle)

Ogorki Kiszone
(Polish Sour Cucumber Pickle)

Peru Che Lonche
(Guava Pickle)

Pickled Armenian Cucumbers
and Gherkins

Panamanian Fried Pickles

Achari Angoor
(Indian Grape Pickle)

Amla Pickle
(Indian Gooseberry Pickle)

Egyptian Pickled Tomatoes

Belgian Chopped Onion and
Cauliflower Pickle

Aloo ko Achar
(Nepalese Potato Pickle)

Bulgarian Pickled Zucchini

Cambodian Pickled Fruit

Aam ka Achar
(Indian Mango Pickle)

Gobhi, Shalgam aur Gajar ka Achar
(Cauliflower, Turnip and
Carrot Pickle)

Nimbu ka Achar
(Vintage Lemon Pickle)

Kachi Haldi ka Achar
(Raw Turmeric Pickle)

Red Chilli Stuffed Pickle

Kerala Prawn Pickle

Amla Murabba
(Gooseberry Sweet Preserve)

Chilli Pineapple Pickle

54 AMLA PICKLE (INDIAN GOOSEBERRY PICKLE)

Amla or gooseberry, as we all know, is good for health. I remember my mother fussing over the amla juice every morning before we left for school. She used to say it would build immunity, and cold and fever would stay miles away.

With the pandemic, we have all realized the importance of those fruits and vegetables that build immunity and act as immunity boosters. Here is a tasty and healthy amla pickle recipe that you can eat with every meal.

Ingredients

200 gm gooseberries/amla
1 tsp turmeric
1 tsp sea salt
½ tsp asafoetida
1 tsp mustard oil
2 tbsp water

Method

In a pan, heat oil and seasoning.

Add in the gooseberries and sauté for 2 minutes.

Add water, cover the lid and reduce the heat to low until the berries are tender.

Remove from heat and bring to room temperature.

Store in the fridge for a month.

55 KERALA MALTA PICKLE

Malta lemon, also called sweet lime or mausambi in Hindi, is a citrus lemon family fruit. It's a fruit that is also used to make fresh juice in summer for hydration. The fruit is rich in vitamin C and fibre, and provides immunity to the body.

The pickle made from Malta lemons is sweet and sour. This is a special pickle from Kerala and one can enjoy it with rice or Indian flatbreads, and even dosa and idli.

Ingredients

4 Malta lemons
3 tsp red chilli flakes
4 green chillies, slit
2 tsp organic jaggery
2 tsp fenugreek seeds
1 1-inch piece ginger, finely chopped
1 tsp asafoetida
2 tsp mustard seeds

2 sprigs curry leaves
2 tbsp refined oil
2 tsp sea salt
1 tsp rock salt

Method

Wash and pat dry the Malta lemons.

Cut into small pieces and boil in water until tender.

Cut green chillies in discs.

Heat oil in a heavy-bottomed pan.

Add mustard and fenugreek seeds and fry until they splutter.

Add curry leaves, ginger, green chilli and sauté for 1 minute.

Add red chilli flakes, salts, jaggery and asafoetida.

Add boiled lemons to 1 cup of water and mix thoroughly.

Adjust water, if needed.

Allow to cool and keep the jar in the balcony or terrace in the sun for a day or two.

Refrigerate for use.

56 BADIMJAN TURSHU (STUFFED AND PICKLED EGGPLANT—AZERBAIJAN)

The word *turshu* is derived from the Persian word *torsh*, which means 'sour'. Turshu may be served as an appetizer that is part of a meze or even alone and as a side dish too. There are many varieties of turshu in Azerbaijan, such as garlic, cabbage, bell peppers, green tomatoes and fruits. One of the most popular is the stuffed and pickled eggplant, which they call Badimjan Turshu in Azerbaijan.

Ingredients

15 medium eggplants
10 garlic cloves
100 gm parsley
1 bunch cilantro
1 cup mint leaves
1 red bell pepper

1 green bell pepper
1 cup basil
⅓ cup salt
1½ cups white vinegar
1½ cups water
½ tsp turmeric

Method

Wash and dry the eggplants.

Remove the stems and do not peel them.

Cut a long slit lengthwise ensuring you do not cut too deep so as to sever the eggplant.

Rub salt inside the eggplants and let it rest for 2 hours to remove the bitterness and excess water.

In a pot of salted water, blanch the eggplants after adding turmeric.

Make sure not to boil them for more than 10 minutes.

Remove from the water and keep in a colander to let the excess water drip.

Place them on a dry surface and press with a heavy plate to drain excess moisture for at least 6–8 hours.

For Filling

Wash and dry all the herbs and finely chop them.

Chop the garlic cloves and mince them in a food processor.

Remove the core and finely chop both red and green peppers.

Add in the herbs, minced garlic and chopped peppers together with salt and 2 spoons of vinegar.

Carefully stuff the herb mixture in the slit eggplants and place them horizontally in the sterilized glass jars so that they do not open up.

Brine

In a pan, heat the vinegar, water and salt for about 10 minutes.

Pour the hot pickling solution over the eggplants in the jars.

Tap the jars to remove air bubbles and seal them.

Store them in a cool place for 4 weeks.

Slice the pickled aubergines before serving.

You can sprinkle them with feta cheese or brush with some olive oil.

Once opened, store in the refrigerator.

57 EGYPTIAN LEMON PICKLE WITH BLACK CUMIN

Egypt—an ancient civilization—is a country of unique cuisine and delicious flatbreads, mezes, pickles, smoky fresh kebabs, scented rice dishes and exquisite desserts. Let's try an ancient lemon pickle recipe from this beautiful and enchanting country of pyramids and mummies.

Ingredients

½ tsp safflowers or saffron thread
2 tbsp cumin seeds
1 tsp peppercorns
1 tbsp rock salt
1 tsp sea salt
½ tsp asafoetida
1 tsp granulated palm sugar
1 cup water

1½ tbsp nigella seeds
6–8 fresh lemons

Method

Wash and pat dry the lemons.

Cut into quarters.

In a saucepan, heat water with salt and lemon, making sure it does not simmer.

Remove from fire.

Drain water and reserve.

In a sterilized jar, squeeze in the lemons, sprinkle peppercorns, safflowers, nigella seeds, sugar, asafoetida and cumin seeds over them and rub well.

Add salty water to cover the lemons completely.

Seal the jar with a non-metal lid and store in a dark place for 2–3 weeks. You can ferment it for a longer duration depending upon your palate.

Once ready, they can be refrigerated until consumed.

58 EGYPTIAN PICKLED TOMATOES

Egyptian tomato pickle is refreshing in summers with its lemony and herbal flavours, soothing and gentle enough to be served as a side dish to strike a balance with a heavy main course. Even as a snack, it is delightful. I normally have it at breakfast with my eggs and toast as it is very energizing. I like to sprinkle some feta cheese and oregano on them.

Ingredients

8–10 ripe, firm red tomatoes
Zest of 1 lemon
8 garlic cloves, minced
2 tsp sea salt
½ cup fresh cilantro, chopped
2 tsp cumin powder
½ cup fresh parsley, chopped
2 tsp black pepper, coarsely ground
8 tbsp white vinegar

½ green bell pepper, chopped
2 tbsp arugula leaves, chopped
½ cup + ½ tbsp extra virgin olive oil
Juice of 2 fresh lemons

Method

In a bowl, mix cilantro, parsley, lemon juice, lemon zest, cumin, salt, black pepper, garlic, chopped green bell pepper and ½ tbsp olive oil and keep aside.

Cut the tomatoes in four diagonal incisions starting at the top, ensuring not to sever them.

Dip each tomato one by one in the marinade to enable them to absorb the marinade.

Pour ½ cup olive oil over the tomatoes and keep aside in a shallow tray.

Keep in the refrigerator for 2 hours before serving.

Sprinkle arugula leaves before serving.

If required, garnish with parsley and cilantro.

59 EGYPTIAN PICKLED AUBERGINES

A very popular Egyptian aubergine pickle. It's a wonderful snack and is great on the meze platter and even as a side dish.

Try this famous Egyptian pickle at home; everyone will enjoy it.

Ingredients

500 gm thin, long aubergines
1 tsp salt
½ red bell pepper, chopped
½ yellow bell pepper, chopped
1 green hot pepper
5 garlic cloves
1 tsp cumin seeds, roasted and ground
3 tsp fresh green coriander, chopped
2 tbsp white vinegar
1 tsp chilli flakes
1 tsp brown sugar

100 gm ripe cherry tomatoes
⅓ cup olives
1 tsp rock salt
1 tsp oregano
Juice of 2 fresh lemons
4 tbsp olive oil

Method

Blanch the aubergines with stalks for 10 minutes.

Remove from water and allow them to cool to room temperature.

In a food processor, blend all the remaining ingredients, other than coriander and oregano, coarsely for stuffing the aubergines.

Once cool, slit the aubergines half way deep, ensuring not to sever them.

Open gently to fill in 1–2 tsp of the stuffing and keep overnight.

Drizzle lemon juice and olive oil over them and garnish with chopped fresh coriander and oregano before serving.

Marinate cherry tomatoes with olive oil and rock salt and serve along with it.

Try sprinkling it with some feta cheese or drizzling some pesto over it.

60 KAZAKHSTANI PICKLED CUCUMBER AND DILL

It was our silver wedding anniversary when we visited Kazakhstan for the first time. Almaty was breathtaking with its snow-clad peaks and airway trolleys ferrying skiers to and fro.

I vividly remember a chilly morning when we had taken a ski trip to one of the highest, freezing peaks. There was a vodka point at 13,000 feet above sea level into which we rushed after a snowy experience, to ward off the cold with a shot of vodka. It was in the tavern that we experienced this exquisite dill and cucumber pickle infused with vodka. Let's try some.

Ingredients

1 kg small cucumbers
1½ tbsp sea salt
1 whole red chilli

4 cups water
1 cup vinegar
8 garlic cloves
1 tbsp raw honey
3 leafy celery sprigs
12 peppercorns
2 dill stalks with flowers
Lime-infused vodka as per serving of the pickle
4–5 horseradish leaves

Method

Mix water and vinegar and add salt, garlic cloves, raw honey, celery and peppercorns, and bring the brine to a boil. Leave it to cool to room temperature.

Wash and pat dry the cucumbers, and cut into spears.

In a sterilized jar, add horseradish at the bottom, pack all the cucumbers and add red chilli and dill stalks at the top.

Mix with all the other ingredients, fill the brine till the top and seal the jar.

Leave on the kitchen shelf for about 48 hours.

Taste the pickle by taking a little out with a sterilized fork.

If you like the taste and it is pleasantly sour, refrigerate it to slow the fermentation process.

Before serving, add a dash of vodka.

61 BELGIAN CHOPPED ONION AND CAULIFLOWER PICKLE

Think of Belgium and you will be reminded of delicious Belgian chocolates. But wait a minute, we are writing about pickles and if you want to make desserts, please refer to my book *On the Dessert Trail.*

Here, we are talking about a national, or should I say, immensely popular Belgian cauliflower pickle. Give this tasty pickle a chance and you will not regret it. You may even wind up with a Belgian liquor dark chocolate after it. Hmmm!

Ingredients

1½ cups white pearl onions
2 cups cauliflower, broken in florets
4 stiff cucumbers, halved
1 whole red chilli
3 tbsp sea salt
1½ cups white vinegar

½ cup coconut sugar
1 tsp turmeric powder
2 tsp mustard powder
1 tsp cornflour
1 tsp pink peppercorns
1 sterilized jar

Method

Clean and dry all the cauliflower, peeled onions and halved cucumbers.

In a bowl, mix coconut sugar, turmeric, cornflour and mustard powder, and add 4–5 tbsp vinegar to make a paste.

Boil water and salt in a non-reactive pan and add the remaining vinegar. Remove from heat.

Rub the vinegar paste on all the vegetables thoroughly.

In a jar, add all the vegetables and the whole red chilli and pink peppercorns.

Pour the brine till the top.

Seal the jar, keep in a warm place in the kitchen for 4 days and then refrigerate for use.

62 AFRICAN BIRD'S EYE PICKLE

As the name suggests, we are going to making a fiery chilli pickle. My mouth is already watering at the thought of eating it with my chia seed bread oozing with mayo and greens, and topped with the bird's eye pickle. I call it my birdie sandwich.

Africa is known for its diversity and exquisite, spicy cuisine. This pickle is one of their most popular pickles.

Ingredients

500 gm bird's eye red chilli peppers
100 gm garlic cloves, minced
1 tbsp coriander seeds
1 tbsp cumin seeds
1 tbsp fenugreek seeds
½ tsp black mustard seeds
2 tbsp salt
1½ cups vinegar
1 tbsp lemon juice

2 tbsp sugar
1 cup water

Method

Bring water and salt to a boil.

Add vinegar, sugar and lemon juice.

Add the roasted spices.

Add the sundried red chilli peppers and garlic cloves.

Top up with the hot brine and seal the jar.

Keep for 48 hours at room temperature.

Store it in the refrigerator.

63 ESTONIAN PICKLED FISH

A recipe from a dear friend from this small Baltic island. Her grandmother passed it on to her and I was fortunate enough to get this from her. My friend told me that her grandmother was so fond of this particular pickle that it was smuggled to the hospital while she was recovering from a long illness, as she would not eat food without it.

Ingredients

5 kg red herring fillets
5 tbsp sugar
1 tbsp salt
1 tsp black pepper, coarsely ground
3 garlic cloves
3 cups water
1 tsp cloves
½ tsp red chilli flakes
2 sprigs thyme

4 bay leaves
1 tsp yellow mustard seeds
1 tsp black peppercorns
2 small yellow onions, sliced
1½ cups white vinegar
1 tsp pickling spice (recipe on page 3)

Method

Place the fish fillets in a pan and pour water to immerse the fish.

Cover and keep overnight. Drain the water in the morning.

Peel and slice the onions.

Pour 3 cups of water in a pan. Add salt, sugar, black pepper, mustard seeds, bay leaves, peppercorns, cloves, red chilli flakes and thyme, and cook for 5 minutes.

Remove from heat, add onions and garlic, and allow it to cool.

Add vinegar and pickling spice and stir.

Pack the herring fillets in the sterilized jars and top up with brine and onion slices.

Seal the jar and store the pickle in the fridge for 5 days before use.

64 LATVIAN PICKLED CUCUMBER

Every region or country has its own unique cucumber pickle recipes. Latvian pickled cucumber with dill and garlic is unique and one of my favourites.

Ingredients

1 kg cucumbers
2 whole fresh red chillies
6 tbsp sea salt
7 cups water
2 cups white vinegar
8 dill stalks with flowers
8 garlic cloves
6 blackcurrant or cherry leaves
1 1-inch piece horseradish shoot

Method

Boil the water with salt.

Cool and add vinegar.

In sterilized jars, add garlic cloves, horseradish, blackcurrant or cherry leaves and dill stalks.

Pack in the cucumbers and insert the red chillies. Top it up with hot brine.

Seal them and the fermentation will start.

Let them be in a dark, cool place for 4–5 days and then refrigerate until consumed.

65 SIBERIAN PICKLED VEGETABLES

Siberia has an extreme cold climate, which makes availability of vegetables very difficult in winter months. So naturally, they bank on preserved vegetables and pickles.

Here is one of Siberia's favourite pickle recipes.

Ingredients

½ large zucchini
1 large onion
½ cauliflower head
4 garlic cloves
6 stiff medium cucumbers
1 dill stem with flowers
2 tbsp mint leaves
1½ litres water
3 tbsp salt
6 peppercorns

2 whole fresh red chillies
½ cup vinegar
6 tsp pickling spice (recipe on page 3)

Method

Sterilize a glass jar.

Wash and clean the vegetables.

Cut cucumbers with skin in discs.

Chop dill, mint, cauliflower and zucchini.

Cut onion in rings.

Place cucumbers, onion, dill, garlic, peppercorns and other vegetables in the jar.

In a pan, pour water and mix salt, and set it to boil.

Remove from heat and add vinegar.

Add pickling spice and pour hot brine in the jar over the vegetables.

Seal and let it rest overnight.

Refrigerate and serve.

66 CHILERO
(NICARAGUAN PICKLE)

Nicaragua, set between the Pacific Ocean and the Caribbean Sea, is a Central American nation known for its dramatic terrain of lakes, volcanoes and beaches. Gallo Pinto is its national dish (rice with black beans and spices, enjoyed with chilero pickle). Although I have never been to this exotic nation, I have friends in America who made me try this super tasty combination.

Ingredients

3 cups white vinegar
2 cups water
2 dried red chillies
1 tbsp granulated sugar
2 garlic cloves, peeled and sliced
2¼ cauliflower, diced into small florets

4 jalapeños, thinly sliced
½ red bell pepper, chopped
2 carrots, thinly sliced
1 medium yellow onion, thinly sliced
1 tbsp salt
1 tsp rock salt
1 tbsp lime juice

Method

In a non-reactive saucepan, bring the water and vinegar mixed with salt and sugar to a boil.

Add the vegetables and lime juice, and remove from heat. Allow it to rest for 1 hour.

Gently transfer to a sterilized glass jar.

All vegetables should be immersed fully in the brine and sealed tightly.

Keep refrigerated until ready to use.

67 ESCABECHE
(GUATEMALAN PICKLED JALAPEÑOS)

Pickled jalapeños, or escabeche, are served as a condiment with many meals in Mexico. Chillies, onions, carrots and cauliflower are pickled with the jalapeños. Crunchy pickled escabeche can be eaten as a snack or appetizer, or served alongside Mexican dishes.

Ingredients

⅓ cup extra virgin olive oil
12 whole jalapeño peppers, a small slit cut in the side of each
2 yellow onions, thickly sliced
1 carrot, peeled and sliced into discs
4 garlic cloves, peeled
½ cup apple cider vinegar
2 tbsp sea salt
2 bay leaves
½ tsp dried oregano

1 tsp fresh oregano
2 fresh thyme sprigs
1½ tbsp sugar
4 black peppercorns

Method

Wash the jalapeño peppers. Cut a cross in the tip end of each chilli leaving the stem intact, so that the vinegar is able to penetrate the chillies.

Heat the oil in a medium-sized, non-reactive saucepan over medium flame.

Add the peppers, carrot, onion and garlic, and sauté for about 4 or 5 minutes until the onion is translucent. Do not brown.

Add the vinegar, salt, bay leaves, fresh and dried oregano, thyme and sugar, and bring to a boil.

Lower the heat and simmer for 10 minutes.

Pack the sterilized jars with the chillies, fried vegetables and peppercorns.

Add pickling brine as needed to bring the liquid to about ½ inch below the rim.

Once opened, you can keep it for about 2 months in the refrigerator.

68 THAI CHILLI REFRIGERATOR PICKLE

One of my favourite destinations, not because of what you are thinking, but because of its exotic cuisine and beaches. I can happily declare it's my favourite cuisine after Indian cuisine. I can eat it daily and never get bored as I love tangy and spicy dishes. This pickle is hot and tangy. Try it!

Ingredients

6 medium stiff Kirby pickling cucumbers, cut into 6 spears
4 bird's eye chilli peppers, slit but not separated
1 cup rice wine vinegar
1 tbsp lime juice
⅓ cup cilantro, chopped
2 tbsp granulated sugar
1 tsp sea salt
3 garlic cloves, peeled and chopped
1 small white onion, sliced

1 tsp Sriracha or any chilli sauce
1 tbsp fresh mint leaves, chopped

Method

Pack the sterilized glass jars with cucumber spears and insert chilli peppers in between the cucumber spears.

In a bowl, combine the rice wine vinegar, lime juice, chilli sauce, onion slices, garlic cloves, cilantro, mint, sugar and salt. Pour over the cucumbers.

Screw a lid on the jar, invert the jar and give it a good shake.

Refrigerate for at least 24 hours before eating.

Enjoy with steamed jasmine rice and Thai curry—yummmmy!

69 ALOO KO ACHAR
(NEPALESE POTATO PICKLE)

Nepali Aloo ko Achar (potato pickle) is very popular and easy to make. It's a versatile pickle that can be used as a condiment, side dish or even a main dish. Although there are many variations of this Nepalese pickle, the basic ingredients are pretty much the same in all recipes, though the consistency of the gravy may vary. You can add sliced cucumber, carrots and even onion as per your preference. We have many Nepalese chefs in our Moti Mahal restaurants. It was from Chef Ramu, who has been with us for umpteen years, that I learnt this recipe.

Ingredients

750 gm potatoes (aloo)
1 yellow onion, sliced
⅓ cup white sesame seeds
½ cup mustard oil

1 tbsp ginger
½ tsp fenugreek seeds
2 tbsp red chilli powder
1 tsp organic turmeric powder
1 tsp timur (Nepalese pungent spice)/Sichuan pepper
3 tbsp lemon juice
⅔ cup water
1 tbsp sea salt
3 green chillies
½ cup fresh coriander, chopped
¼ tsp asafoetida

Method

Parboil the potatoes, peel them and cut in small cubes or discs.

Roast sesame seeds till light brown.

Slit the green chillies and grind the timur spice.

In a bowl, mix the potatoes, timur, sesame seeds, green chillies, onion slices, salt, chilli powder and turmeric powder and mix well.

Heat oil in a wok.

Add fenugreek seeds and cook until they splutter.

Add asafoetida and ginger.

Lower the heat, add the potato mix and stir to mix.

Add lemon juice, water and chopped coriander.

Cover the pan with a lid and let it cook until water evaporates.

Keep aside for about 1 hour.

Refrigerate and keep giving it a stir in between.

It can be stored for 1 month.

70 TURCHI TARKARI
(AFGHANI VEGETABLE PICKLE)

I have heard many tales about Kabul as my maternal grandfather hailed from there and was in the dry fruit business. Whenever I would visit their home with my mother and siblings, we would eat Kabuli food with Afghani vegetable pickle, which my grandmother used to make. It's the most popular Afghani pickle with some exotic spices.

Ingredients

100 gm small aubergines
100 gm carrots, diced
100 gm cauliflower, cut in florets
100 gm turnips
50 gm cucumber, diced
50 gm yellow bell peppers
50 gm red bell peppers
2 cups white vinegar

Zest of 1 lemon
10 hot green chillies
10 garlic cloves, peeled
2 tbsp sea salt
1 tsp dry mint powder
1 tbsp nigella seeds
2 cups fresh coriander, chopped

Method

Chop and boil all the vegetables for about 5 minutes until tender.

Place all the vegetables in sterilized glass jars.

In a blender, add chopped coriander, lemon zest, green chillies sparing 2 or 3, and garlic with vinegar.

Blend well.

Top the jars with green chillies.

Add sea salt, nigella seeds and dry mint on top of the vegetables.

Pour the vinegar mixture till the brim and seal the jars for 2–3 days.

Refrigerate and use within 2 months.

71 CZECH SWEET AND SOUR PICKLE

A few years ago, when we visited Prague for a holiday, I was not only intrigued by its beauty but enchanted by its delicious cuisine.

The Czech Republic has a very traditional meat and potato cuisine, usually with gravies, stew, meat loaf (made with pork and beef), goulash, garlic-heavy soup with croutons, česnečka and karbanátek (meat patty crumbed and deep fried and called a burger). I clearly remember that summer as there was flooding and we had to remain indoors because the water had come right up the streets. It was on one of those afternoons that I tried this pickle with meat loaf and soup. It is truly a delicious pickle.

Ingredients

6 cups water
2½ cups white vinegar
2 cups salt

10 medium stiff pickling cucumbers, quartered or halved lengthwise
4 dill sprigs or heads
8 garlic cloves
4 dried hot chillies
¼ cup brown sugar
½ tsp turmeric powder
½ tsp yellow mustard seeds

Method

Soak cucumbers in water with salt overnight.

In a non-reactive pan, heat water, vinegar, brown sugar and salt, and bring it to a boil for 10 minutes.

Take 2 sterilized jars and pack them with 5 cucumbers each, and 2 dill heads, 4 garlic cloves and 2 dried red chillies on top, per jar.

Carefully pour hot brine over the cucumbers and ensure they are fully immersed.

Add ¼ tsp yellow mustard seeds and ¼ tsp turmeric powder in each jar.

When the brine comes down to room temperature, seal the jars tightly with their lids.

Give the jars a hot water bath for about 15 minutes.

Remove and let the jars cool down.

Store in the fridge for use. It can stay for about 2 months.

72 BULGARIAN PICKLED ZUCCHINI

Pickled zucchini is very popular in Bulgaria. Zucchini is a very versatile vegetable, which provides an earthy flavour to the dish. It can be eaten raw in salads, steamed or sautéed as per the requirement of your recipe.

This tangy Bulgarian pickle is best consumed as a part of your cheeseboard, salads or meze platter.

Ingredients

8 zucchini, sliced
2 tbsp sea salt
1 bunch dill stalks
4 blackcurrants
4 cherries
5 cups apple cider vinegar
3 cups caster sugar
2 tsp brown mustard seeds
2 tsp coriander seeds

1 bunch celery
2 tsp mustard powder
2 tsp turmeric powder
½ cup parsley, chopped

Method

Place the zucchini in a large bowl with 2 tbsp sea salt and mix with a toss.

Cover with iced water and leave to brine for about half an hour.

Drain and keep the zucchini aside.

Pour vinegar, sugar and spices in a large non-reactive saucepan, place over medium heat and bring to a boil.

Reduce heat to low and simmer for 2–3 minutes.

Turn off the heat and stir in some of the parsley and celery.

Put the brined zucchini in a clean sterilized jar, pressing the mixture down so it is firmly packed.

Add the dill stalks, the rest of the parsley, cherries and blackcurrants in the jar.

Pour the pickling liquid over this and seal tightly with the lid.

Store in the fridge and use for about 2 months.

73 SPANISH HOT GUINDİLLA PEPPERS

The Guindilla chilli pepper is grown and processed in the Basque region of Spain. The word *guindilla* translates to 'chilli pepper' in English. It is narrow and long with a mild heat level and is usually pickled. During my trip to Spain, while I was in Madrid, the chef of the hotel made a fried chilli sandwich for me with these pepper pickles, as I had requested him to make me a spicy snack to satiate my Indian palate. Later, on request, I learnt this recipe from him.

Ingredients

1 kg chillies/Spanish guindilla peppers
10 garlic cloves, peeled
1 tbsp pickling spice (recipe on page 3)
¼ tsp mustard seeds
5–6 peppercorns
2 cardamom pods
¼ tsp fenugreek seeds

2 cups vinegar
1 tbsp sugar
1 tsp sea salt
2 sprigs thyme
½ tsp nigella seeds

Method

Cut the chillies in roundels or make a lengthwise incision without severing them.

In a non-reactive pan, heat vinegar, salt and sugar, and boil for 10 minutes.

Add the spices and condiments to the brine.

In a jar, stuff the chillies with garlic cloves and thyme.

Pour the brine over the chillies leaving 1 inch space at the top.

Shake the jar to remove the air bubbles and seal with its lid tightly.

Store in a dark place overnight and then keep them in the fridge for use up to 2 months.

74 BARBADIAN PICKLED CUCUMBER

This is a simple Barbadian pickled cucumber recipe. It's zesty and refreshingly light. This humble pickle is quite versatile as it makes a great side and even complements heavy main dishes that need lime juice to lighten up the meal with a little heat generated from the hot scotch bonnet pepper.

Ingredients

5 stiff cucumbers, Barbadian
½ medium onion, minced finely
¼ tsp sugar
1 tbsp mint leaves, crushed
2 tsp sea salt
½ scotch bonnet pepper, minced finely
1 tsp vinegar
4 tsp fresh lime juice
1 small bunch parsley, chopped

Method

Wash and clean the cucumbers.

Soak them in salted water overnight and drain in the morning.

Cut them in roundels.

Mix lime juice and vinegar together, along with sugar and seasoning.

Drizzle over cucumbers and onions, and mix well.

Garnish with chopped parsley and mint leaves.

In my twist, I add a teaspoon of sesame seed oil in lime juice and vinegar.

Serve chilled.

75 UKRAINIAN DILL AND GARLIC PICKLE

During my show at the Paris Cookbook Fair where I was demonstrating how to cook biryani, I met Sofia, a Ukrainian schoolteacher who had come to witness my demo. I still remember I was speaking about the medicinal values of garlic and how we should incorporate it in our daily diet. Sofia was gracious enough to share this garlic pickle recipe with the audience during the show.

Ingredients

2 kg small stiff pickling cucumbers
16 cups water
⅔ cup kosher salt
½ cup garlic heads, cloves separated and peeled, sliced
2 grape leaves
6 peppercorns
2 fresh red chilli peppers, sliced
1 bunch dill stalks with flowers

Method

Soak cucumbers in cold salted water overnight.

Drain the water in the morning and prepare the cucumbers by trimming the sides and making a slit lengthwise.

Boil water with salt.

Sterilize the jars and place half of the garlic slices, peppercorns, dill, grape leaves and sliced red peppers at the bottom of each jar.

Push half the cucumbers into the jar and then repeat the layers.

Pour boiling brine into the packed jar immersing the cucumbers in it and cover with the lid tightly.

Store for 5 days or until they have fermented to suit your palate.

Refrigerate for use.

76 TORSHI SHOOR
(IRANIAN PICKLED VEGETABLES)

Torshi are vegetables that are pickled in brine, seen in the cuisines of several countries in the Balkans and the Middle East, as well as Arab countries. Persia was the cultural hub in the olden days with art, cuisine and literature at its peak. My grandfather, who hailed from the North-west Frontier, was fluent in Pashto (Persian language) and being a chef and the owner of the renowned restaurant Moti Mahal, he would keenly follow Persian recipes. This mixed vegetable pickle was always kept ready in our home kitchen as he would say it is not only tasty but healthy. I remember fussing over eating vegetables during my meals, so he would give me this tangy vegetable pickle rolled up in crisp Indian tandoori flatbreads with white homemade butter, which I would relish.

Ingredients

3 celery sticks
1 large carrot, washed, peeled and chopped
3 eggplants, peeled and sliced
1 stiff cucumber, chopped
3 small onions, sliced
½ cabbage
4 red chilli peppers
½ cup cauliflower
4 garlic cloves
3 jalapeño peppers
1 tbsp mint
1 tbsp basil
1 tbsp tarragon
2 tbsp coriander seeds
1 tbsp sea salt
1 tsp turmeric
1½ cups white vinegar

Method

Place the sliced eggplants in a pot and mix in vinegar with water.

Heat the pot for 6–7 minutes.

Clean and dry all the herbs.

In a mixing bowl, add all the ingredients, including cooked eggplants in brine and mix well.

Using a wooden ladle, put all the vegetables in sterilized jars large enough to accommodate the pickle.

Top up with vinegar as required and add salt on the top before sealing each jar tightly.

Store for at least 3 weeks before serving.

Keep it in the refrigerator until consumed.

77 TORSHI SEER
(IRANIAN PICKLED GARLIC)

As the name suggests, *torshi seer* in Persian means 'sour garlic' or 'garlic pickle'. It is very popular in Iran and other Arabian and Mediterranean countries.

This pickle is especially healthy as garlic is good for health and since it is fermented, it becomes even more healthy and tastier. It works great in antipasti or meze platters. Just put some cream cheese on lavash with some torshi seer—it's divine.

Ingredients

6 garlic heads, break into cloves with skin
1½ cups balsamic, malt, cider or white vinegar
1 cup red wine vinegar
2 tbsp raw honey
¼ cup dried barberries
2 tsp salt
3 fresh thyme sprigs

Method

Place garlic in a sterilized glass jar and set aside.

Bring balsamic and red wine vinegar, barberries, honey, salt and thyme to a boil in a non-reactive saucepan.

Pour over the garlic, place a lid on the jar, and let it cool to room temperature.

Store in a cool, dark place for at least 6 weeks before serving.

The longer you ferment the pickle, the more it will melt in your mouth.

78 CAMBODIAN PICKLED FRUIT

Pickled fruits are very popular in Cambodia. Many varieties of fruits, such as green papaya, green mango, green plums, sour grapes, etc., can be used. But my favourites are green plums or unripe, sour green grapes pickles.

One can eat them as sides or as an accompaniment with main courses. I love to eat it with steamed rice and basil stir-fry vegetables with bamboo shoots and tofu.

Ingredients

⅓ cup kosher salt
1 tsp pink peppercorns
2 tbsp sugar
3 cups water
1 kg green plums

Method

In a pan, heat water, sugar and salt together.

Bring to a boil and then cool.

In a sterilized glass jar, stuff the green plums plus peppercorns and pour the pickling brine up to the rim, ensuring that the plums are submerged in the brine.

Seal the jar tightly with the lid and store for 2–4 days depending upon the fermenting or sourness you require.

Once satisfied with the sourness, refrigerate until consumed.

79 TAIWANESE PICKLED CABBAGE

On my recent visit to Taiwan, I discovered pork is a predominant ingredient, often showing up in a family-style platter to start the meal. I had gone for dinner with a friend to a seaside hotel where he treated me to the local sweet and sour pork, which was served with the popular cabbage pickle and, of course, steamed jasmine rice. The combo was magical.

I have always enjoyed my coleslaw burgers, but pickled cabbage is something else. So here we go with this magical pickle recipe. It's a great accompaniment to any barbeque dish. I tried it with tandoori chicken and paneer tikka and warm parantha, and my mouth is still watering!

Ingredients

500 gm stiff cabbage, cut into bite sizes
1 large carrot, peeled and cut in discs
4 red chilli peppers
½ cup organic rice vinegar

4 tbsp sugar
1 tbsp kosher salt
3 garlic cloves, smashed
1 1-inch piece ginger, peeled and sliced
1 cup water

Method

Rub salt on cabbage and carrot and keep aside.

Wash the carrot and cabbage and drain well.

Make the pickling brine by mixing water, vinegar, salt and sugar, bring it to a boil and allow it to cool.

Place the cabbage and carrot along with chilli peppers, garlic and ginger in a sterilized glass jar and pour brine to cover the vegetables.

Seal with a lid and store in the fridge overnight before serving.

80 VIETNAMESE CARROT AND DAIKON PICKLE

Vietnamese carrot and daikon refrigerator pickle is also known as 'do chua'. I sparingly use this Vietnamese pickle in many dishes. It is commonly eaten with a Vietnamese sandwich called banh mi. The root vegetables are cut, brined and can be eaten almost immediately. Their flavours will deepen with a few days in the refrigerator and they can be enjoyed as you would any pickled vegetable.

Daikon radishes are very large, over a foot long, white, mild radishes. Carrots were added to bring colour to this pickle. It is not cooked, so it is a refrigerator pickle, not 'canned'.

Ingredients

4 large carrots, peeled
2 large daikon radishes, peeled
5 tsp and 1 cup granulated sugar

5 tsp sea salt
2½ cups white vinegar
2 cups water
1 large whole red chilli

Method

Julienne the carrots and the daikon radishes.

Rub with 5 tsp sugar and salt and leave in a large bowl.

Transfer the carrots and daikon to a colander, rinse with cool water and drain well.

In a bowl, mix together one cup of sugar, the white vinegar and warm water, until the sugar dissolves.

Stuff the daikon and carrots in a sterilized jar and pour the pickling brine over it, add red chilli on top.

Seal the jar with its lid and refrigerate overnight, shaking it whenever possible.

Store for about 3–5 weeks.

81 KISELI LUPUS
(CROATIAN SOURED CABBAGE HEADS)

A scenic island country with breathtaking views, Croatia is situated in Central and South-east Europe, and has European cuisine.

We flew to Croatia from Turkey and landed at Zagreb. We toured the entire country, basking in the sun at beaches and diving in cool blue waters, in a land where it seemed that time had come to a halt. The rich Croatian culture is a mix of traditions drawn from Greek and Roman civilizations, which influenced their cuisines, music, architecture and art.

Soured cabbage pickle is a very popular Croatian pickle, often used to make cabbage rolls called sarma.

Ingredients

10 bay leaves
2 red bell peppers
12 cabbage heads

1 6-inch piece horseradish root
10 red peppers, dry
3 cups sea salt
6 garlic cloves, chopped

Method

Remove the outer layer of the cabbage.

Core the cabbage heads and fill in sea salt. Press to add more.

Repeat for all the cabbage heads.

In a barrel, put the cabbage heads alternating with the peppers, garlic, bay leaves, salt and dry red peppers.

Place the horseradish root on the top and add water to fill up to the rim.

Put some weight so the cabbage heads don't float.

Seal the lid with a cotton cloth.

Let it ferment for about 40 days; in between, clean the brine solution from the top.

Remove and freeze the heads or can them for later use.

82 AAM KA ACHAR (INDIAN MANGO PICKLE)

An all-time favourite. There are so many variations of making this single pickle that one can write a book only on mango pickle varieties. However, I am sharing the one that was popular in my home and has been made for the last 100 years in my family.

Ingredients

5 kg raw mangoes with tender skin (kachcha aam)
400 gm fenugreek seeds, coarsely ground
275 gm mustard seeds, coarsely ground
475 gm fennel seeds, coarsely ground
6 tsp nigella seeds
5 tbsp red chilli powder (degi mirch)
6 tbsp Kashmiri mirch
11 tsp turmeric
5 tsp asafoetida

550 gm salt
2½ cups mustard oil

Method

Dry the whole spices for a day in bright sunlight to remove the moisture.

Coarsely crush mustard, fennel and fenugreek seeds.

Mix all the spices in a bowl.

Wash and wipe the mangoes with a cloth napkin.

Chop mangoes into medium-size pieces and add some nigella seeds.

In a big Mason jar, add the chopped mango pieces and spices, all the powdered spices and salt.

Mix well with a wooden ladle so all the mango pieces are evenly coated with spices.

Heat the oil till its smoking point and then remove from heat.

Pour over the mangoes and shake the jar so the oil can filter in.

Mix well and cover the bowl with a muslin cloth.

Keep in sunlight during the day and store inside at night for about a week or more as per your fermentation preference.

Open the lid daily and give the pickle a shake.

With a clean wooden ladle, move the pickle so as to get the mangoes at the bottom to the top. Repeat daily until the pickle matures.

Add the remaining mustard oil to the jar; the oil should be at least 2 inches above the pickle level.

Cover the jar with its lid and let it mature for a week or two before you start using it.

No need to refrigerate it as it stays fresh until it lasts.

83 GOBHI, SHALGAM AUR GAJAR KA ACHAR (CAULIFLOWER, TURNIP AND CARROT PICKLE)

This is a special and all-time, all-season favourite recipe passed on by my mother-in-law, and now my wife makes it. Believe me, it's always in demand from all our relatives and friends. The sweet and sour pickle goes well with breads, rice and main courses.

Ingredients

1 kg organic jaggery (gur)
1 litre mustard oil
1 litre vinegar
200 gm black mustard seeds
250 gm garlic paste
2 kg onion, grated
5 kg cauliflower florets
2 kg turnips, diced

2 kg carrots, peeled and cut in stick shape
2 tbsp turmeric
4 tbsp red chilli powder (degi mirch)
4 tbsp sea salt

Method

Dip vegetables in warm water and dry under a fan.

In a pan, heat mustard oil and switch off the heat.

Bring the oil to room temperature.

In a pan, heat the oil and sauté the garlic paste until it starts sticking to the bottom.

Add all the vegetables and spices.

Add mustard seeds.

Add jaggery and stir until it is fully incorporated in the pickle.

Add vinegar and keep in the sun for about 5–6 days.

Store in an airtight Mason jar.

84 NIMBU KA ACHAR (VINTAGE LEMON PICKLE)

A pickle available in most homes that is treated as a medicine but is delicious enough for you to want to eat this medicine with every meal.

A salted, layered parantha with buttermilk and nimbu ka achar is a killer combination.

Ingredients

250 gm lemon with thin peel
2 tbsp mustard oil
1 tsp white peppercorns
1 tbsp cloves
1 tbsp black peppercorns
1 tbsp red chilli flakes
2 tbsp jaggery
8 black cardamoms
1 tsp carom seeds

½ tsp black salt
½ tsp cardamom powder
½ tsp sea salt

Method

Wash and clean the lemons.

Cut them lengthwise in 4 quarters and keep aside.

In a blender, grind black cardamom, black and white peppercorns and cloves.

In a pan, heat oil until smoky and add the carom seeds.

Add jaggery and stir until dissolved.

Add the ground spices.

Add the rest of the spices and remove from fire.

Add the lemons and stir for a few minutes until the pickle marinade is fully mixed with the lemons.

Place in a ceramic Mason jar and keep in the sun for about a week.

Keep shaking the jar.

Store in the kitchen for about 2 months and keep stirring and shaking the jar occasionally until it matures.

85 MURG ACHAR (CHICKEN PICKLE)

As the name suggests, it's a tangy chicken pickle made with Indian spices. It's great to eat with steamed rice and tandoori bread (roti).

Ingredients

1 boneless chicken, skinless, cut in 12 pieces
1 tsp fenugreek seeds
1 tsp mustard seeds
1 tsp aniseed
1 tsp cumin seeds
1 tsp nigella seeds
1 tsp Kashmiri mirch (red chilli powder)
1 tsp turmeric powder
6 green chillies
2 tsp garlic paste
1 tsp ginger paste

¼ cup white vinegar
1 tbsp jaggery
1 tbsp lime juice
3 tbsp mustard oil
1 tsp sea salt

Method

Heat oil in a pan, add the fenugreek seeds, mustard seeds, aniseed, cumin seeds and nigella seeds, and sauté till they splutter.

Add ginger paste and garlic paste and sauté until golden brown.

Add red chilli powder and turmeric powder.

Mix in green chillies.

Add jaggery and cook until it melts.

Add chicken pieces and cook on medium heat till they are tender and the oil separates.

Add all spices and salt and mix well over high heat.

Add lime juice.

Add vinegar, bring it to a boil and switch off the heat.

Let it cool and then refrigerate until consumed.

86 KACHI HALDI KA ACHAR (RAW TURMERIC PICKLE)

This immunity booster turmeric pickle is a must for all homes. It contains many bioactive compounds and is a powerhouse of medicinal properties. Turmeric contains curcumin, a substance with powerful anti-inflammatory and antioxidant properties. Turmeric improves brain function and helps reduce brain diseases.

So, give it a try and always keep a ready dose in your fridge to enjoy with your meals.

Ingredients

1 cup fresh turmeric roots
3 tbsp oil
1 tsp black mustard seeds
½ tsp asafoetida
1 tsp pickling spice (recipe on page 3)
1 tsp sea salt

½ tsp carom seeds (optional)
1 tbsp jaggery (optional)

Method

Wash and thoroughly dry the turmeric roots.

Peel and chop them very fine or grate them as per your choice.

Heat the oil and add the mustard seeds and asafoetida. (If using carom and jaggery, add at this stage and stir.)

Stir until the seeds crackle.

Remove from the heat and cool.

Mix the raw turmeric in the cooled spice mix.

Add the pickling spice and salt. Stir well.

Cover and store in the refrigerator.

Note: Never use a wet spoon in the jar as it will cause the pickle to ferment and spoil it.

87 RED CHILLI STUFFED PICKLE

A very popular stuffed Indian pickle. Large red chilli peppers stuffed with roasted spices are irresistible when eaten with paranthas, stuffed in pita bread with vegetables or even in sandwiches.

Ingredients

1 kg large red chilli peppers
50 gm carom seeds
100 gm fennel seeds
100 gm cumin seeds
100 gm fenugreek seeds
100 gm mustard seeds

Seasoning

200 gm sea salt
50 gm dry mango powder

50 gm dry red chilli flakes
100 gm turmeric
1½ litre mustard oil

Method

Clean the whole spices.

Roast carom seeds and fenugreek seeds.

Grind all the seeds, including mustard seeds.

Add all the spices (in the Seasoning list) and give it a shake.

Heat oil and keep aside to cool.

Mix 1 cup oil to make a spice paste for the filling. Adjust the consistency by adding some more oil if needed.

Wash and clean the chilli peppers.

Remove the stalk tips of the peppers with a sharp knife.

Remove the core with the help of a knife without breaking the peppers.

Fill in the spice mixture by pressing gently all the way till the bottom of the chilli.

Repeat the process for all the chilli peppers.

In a sterilized glass Mason jar, start filling the prepared chilli peppers gently, pressing them down all the way to the top.

Reserve 1 inch space at the top.

Pour in the oil and ensure all the peppers are fully immersed and the oil is floating 1 inch above the chilli peppers.

Seal the jar with its lid tightly.

Cover with a cloth and tie with a string.

Keep in the sun for a month.

Once the pickle is ready, store in a cool, dark place in the kitchen.

88 OYSTER MUSHROOM PICKLE

This is a special mushroom pickle that goes well with salads and sandwiches.

Ingredients

200 gm oyster mushrooms
1 tsp salt
1 tsp coriander seeds
1 tsp carom seeds
1 tsp cumin seeds
1 tsp fennel seeds
1 tsp fenugreek seeds
2 tsp black mustard seeds
1 tsp nigella seeds
1 tsp raw mango powder
1 tsp red chilli powder
1 tsp garam masala
1 tsp turmeric

⅓ tsp asafoetida
¼ tsp sodium benzoate
½ tsp sea salt
½ tsp rock salt
400 ml mustard oil

Method

In a pan, bring water to a boil and add salt.

Add mushrooms and stir for 3–5 minutes.

Drain in a colander and wash with cold water a couple of times.

Rub salt on mushrooms and spread over a muslin cloth.

Put under the sun for 2 hours for moisture to evaporate.

In a pan, roast coriander seeds, cumin seeds, fenugreek seeds and carom seeds for 5 minutes and cool them to room temperature. Then, grind them to a powder.

Roast the mustard seeds and nigella seeds for 2 minutes.

Mix all the seeds and spices.

In a pan, put the mushrooms and add the spices and seeds mix.

Add oil in batches to mix well.

Add salt and sodium benzoate.

Put the pickle in a Mason jar and fill with mustard oil.

Seal the jar and put it under the sun for 3 days.

When the pickle is ready, store it in a cool, dark place in the kitchen.

89 KERALA PRAWN PICKLE

Kerala prawn pickle is spicy, packs a punch and is full of flavour. It provides a meaty touch to every meal.

Ingredients

500 gm medium prawns, cleaned and deveined
1 2-inch piece ginger, chopped
15 garlic cloves
1 tsp mustard seeds
¾ cup white vinegar
⅓ cup water
4 tsp Kashmiri chilli powder for colour
2 whole dry red chilli peppers
1½ tsp turmeric powder
2 cups coconut oil for frying
⅓ cup curry leaves
2 green chillies, slit

Method

Take 1 tsp turmeric powder and 1 tsp chilli powder and rub well on the prawns.

Heat the oil in a wok.

Add the prawns and fry until golden brown.

Remove with a slotted ladle.

In a separate pan, add ¾ cup oil which was used for frying with all the residues.

Add mustard seeds, dry red chillies, curry leaves, green chillies, garlic and ginger, and fry for a few minutes until the garlic and ginger turn golden.

Add 3 tsp chilli powder and salt and stir.

Add vinegar and water and cook for 3–4 minutes.

Add the rest of the spices and then the fried prawns, and stir till the gravy thickens.

Remove from fire and bring to room temperature.

Store in a clean jar and refrigerate until consumed.

90 KACHALU ACHAR (COLOCASIA PICKLE)

I have always enjoyed eating this gooey pickle with my poori (fried Indian flat bread) or rice with vegetables. It's a very tasty and tangy pickle.

Ingredients

3 round colocasia (about 700 gm)
2 cups water
3 tsp fennel seeds
1½ tsp fenugreek seeds
1½ tsp salt
1½ tsp red chilli powder (degi mirch)
1 tsp turmeric powder
1½ tsp ground black mustard seeds
1 cup mustard oil
⅓ tsp asafoetida

Method

Add water and colocasia in a pressure cooker and cook on high heat.

Wait for 5 whistles on medium heat.

Remove from fire and let the pressure release on its own from the pressure cooker.

Remove and check by piercing with a knife and seeing if it comes out clean.

Remove the skin and the tips of the colocasia and then cut it into small pieces.

Coarsely grind fennel and fenugreek seeds and mix this in the colocasia.

Add salt, red chilli powder, ground mustard seeds, mustard oil and asafoetida.

Mix all the spices uniformly over the colocasia.

Keep in a sterilized glass jar, seal airtight with its lid and store for a week.

Shake daily for the next week.

Store in a cool, dark place.

SWEET PRESERVES

MURABBAS

For those who don't like pickles, we have a solution. Yes! We can eat sweet options like carrot, gooseberry or apple preserve. They are slightly spiced and cooked in jaggery, sugar or brown sugar and can be preserved in jars and refrigerated for months. They are good for health and tasty. So let's give them a try in our home kitchens.

91 GAJAR MURABBA (CARROT SWEET PRESERVE)

The best way to preserve carrots for summers is in the form of murabba or sweet preserve garnished with nuts. It's healthy, nourishing and very tasty too. I would gulp several pieces in about a minute before going to school. This serves as an energy booster too.

Ingredients

1 kg red carrots
500 gm sugar
1 pinch saffron
½ tsp cardamom powder
Juice of 1 fresh lemon
2–3 silver leaf foil

Method

Wash and clean the carrots. Peel them and remove the yellow part, if any.

Take a deep pan and heat enough water to cover the carrots.

Boil the carrots for 2–3 minutes.

Once the water starts to boil, turn off the flame and cover the pan with a lid. Let it stand for about 5 minutes.

Remove the carrots, put them in a strainer and cover it with a cloth to drain the excess water. Keep the water aside.

Once the water dries from the carrots, pierce holes in them with a fork.

Place the carrots in a steel pan and rub the sugar evenly on all the carrots. Cover with a cloth and leave overnight.

There will be some sugary juice that will come out of the carrots. Collect it and set it aside.

In a heavy-bottomed pan, heat the carrots, drained water and juice residue until a thick, one-string consistency of the sugar syrup is obtained.

Cook the carrots on a low flame and keep stirring. Add cardamom powder and saffron and stir.

Add lemon juice to remove any sugar crystallization on the carrots, remove from fire and let it cool.

Put silver leaf foil over the murabba gently. Store in steel containers.

92 AMLA MURABBA
(GOOSEBERRY SWEET PRESERVE)

Indian gooseberry is rich in vitamin C, promotes the immune system and heart health, supports digestion, improves kidney health and is an antioxidant. You can choose to pickle them or make sweet preserves. I love the sweet preserve as it is a great snack. Of course, it's not just empty calories but is a reservoir of nutrition.

Ingredients

1 kg amla (gooseberries)
2 cups water
2–3 green cardamom seeds, crushed
½ tsp freshly ground black peppercorns
1 pinch rock salt
1 pinch saffron
1½ kg brown sugar or gur (jaggery)
1½ litres water
½ lemon

Method

Wash and clean the amla and soak overnight in water, just enough to cover them. Drain and store the water.

Pierce them all over with a fork. Place the berries in a non-stick pan, add the saved water and cook on a low flame for about 12–15 minutes covered with a lid, until the amla is tender and water is reduced to half the quantity.

Drain the berries and reserve the water in which the amla was cooked.

Heat sugar or jaggery with 1½ litres of water (which includes the reserved water) in a heavy-bottomed pan (non-reactive) until brown sugar or jaggery dissolves completely and forms a syrup of one-string consistency.

Add a few drops of lemon juice to clarify the sugar crystallization. Remove the scum or froth and discard. Strain the sugar syrup through a muslin cloth to further remove the impurities.

Place the sugar syrup again on a low flame, add amla and continue to cook.

Add the crushed green cardamom seeds, ground peppercorn and saffron.

Continue to cook without a lid on a low flame until the mixture is thick and the syrup is of two-string (honey-like) consistency.

Add a pinch of rock salt and mix well.

Cool it completely and store in airtight jars. Ensure that the amla is completely immersed in the syrup while it is stored.

93 SEB KA MURABBA (APPLE SWEET PRESERVE)

Seb is a murabba, as my granny used to call it in her native language. She would prepare it in season, store it and religiously make us eat this delicious preserve. Apple preserve, with its sweet and tangy taste, and hint of cinnamon and cardamom flavours, can be eaten as healthy snack whenever one feels hungry. One can also substitute the brown sugar with jaggery.

Ingredients

1 kg apples
1¼ kg brown sugar
2 tsp lemon juice
½ tsp cardamom powder
2 1-inch cinnamon sticks

Method

Wash and clean the apples; peel and core them.

In a heavy-bottomed, non-reactive pan, heat water and bring it to a boil.

Add apples in the vessel and cook till they become soft. Remove apples from the water.

Add sugar and cinnamon sticks in the water and cook until the sugar syrup becomes thick (honey-like consistency).

Add lemon and cardamom powder.

Add the cooked apples and stir well.

Keep aside for 2–3 days.

Store in an airtight container and refrigerate.

94 GALGAL ACHAR (HILL LEMON PICKLE)

I remember my grandmother used to make this delicious sweet and sour pickle and she would relish it a lot too. She would say, 'One doesn't have to wait for months for this pickle to be ready as this is ready to eat immediately after making it.' Hill lemon or galgal or citron is a large fragrant citrus fruit with a thick rind, widely used in Indian cuisine as well as traditional medicines. It is an indigenous variety of lemon generally grown in north India, especially in the foothills of the lower Himalayas due to its wider adaptability and high-yield potential.

Ingredients

2 hill lemons
2 tsp red chilli powder
1 tsp turmeric powder
4 tbsp mustard oil
1 tsp cumin powder

1 tsp carom seeds
1 tsp fennel seeds
1 tsp fenugreek powder
1 tsp aniseed
1 tsp whole dry red pepper, crushed
1 tbsp sea salt or as per taste
3 tbsp brown sugar

Method

Wash and clean the lemons.

Boil for 5 minutes in water, and keep turning the lemons while boiling.

Let them cool down in the water and remove once the water is at room temperature.

Cut the lemons from the centre, squeeze the juice in a bowl and then cut into small wedges.

In a pan, heat oil, add fennel seeds and carom seeds, and stir till they splutter.

Add lemon juice, aniseed, crushed red pepper, turmeric powder, red chilli powder, cumin powder and mix well.

Add salt and stir.

Add fenugreek powder and sugar, and mix well until the sugar is incorporated.

Add lemons, stir and cook for 2 minutes.

Let it cool to room temperature.

In a sterilized jar, add hill lemons and it's ready to serve.

95 DATE PICKLE

This is one of my favourite pickles with the sweetness of dates and tanginess of tamarind. It goes very well with fritters, samosas and chaat.

Ingredients

100 gm seedless dates, chopped
4–5 tbsp coconut oil
1 tsp mustard seeds
½ tsp fenugreek seeds
12 garlic cloves, finely chopped
1 1-inch piece ginger, grated
4 green chillies, chopped
1 tsp red chilli powder
2 tsp sea salt
½ tsp turmeric powder

¾ cup tamarind purée
1 tbsp jaggery
1 sprig curry leaves

Method

Heat oil in a pan and add mustard seeds and fenugreek seeds. Cook till they splutter.

Add ginger and garlic.

Sauté till light golden brown and then lower the flame to medium.

Add green chillies, curry leaves, turmeric powder and chilli powder.

Add chopped dates and stir for a few minutes.

Add tamarind purée and cook until the mixture is incorporated.

Add salt and stir in jaggery.

Remove from heat and bring it to room temperature.

Store in a jar and refrigerate.

96 KUL/CHINESE DATES/JUJUBE PICKLE

Kul is commonly known as jujubes or red dates. They are high in vitamin C and increase immunity. The pickle is easy and quick to make.

Ingredients

500 gm ripe jujube/kul berries
3 whole dry red chillies
1 tbsp panch phoron masala (recipe on page 8)
1 tbsp fennel seeds
1 tsp coriander seeds
1 tsp cumin seeds
½ cup water
½ tsp sea salt
300 gm organic jaggery

Method

Break the skin of the ripened berries. Discard the overripe or spoilt ones.

Wash under a tap and rinse well.

In a pan, on low heat, roast dry chillies.

Add the seeds and panch phoron spices, and roast for 3 minutes.

Set aside to cool to room temperature.

In a wok, add water and heat it, but do not bring it to a boil.

Add the jaggery and stir on low heat until dissolved.

Cook for 5 minutes till the consistency thickens.

Add the berries and cook for 10 minutes.

Stir in salt and other ingredients, and cook for 3–4 minutes.

Remove and cool to room temperature.

Store in a glass jar and refrigerate until consumed.

97 BEL ACHAR
(WOOD APPLE PICKLE)

This popular Indian fruit is also used in religious ceremonies. In summers, bel sherbet (beverage) is popular in India due to its cooling properties. Let's try a tangy pickle made with this fruit.

Ingredients

4 ripe wood apples
1½ tsp sea salt
¼ cup mustard oil
¼ cup sugar or jaggery
1 tbsp tamarind
1 tsp roasted cumin seeds
1 tbsp panch phoron masala (recipe on page 8)
1 tbsp chilli flakes
1.2 cups fresh lemon juice

Method

In a pan, heat oil.

Break open the wood apples and take out the pulp with a spoon.

Mash the pulp and fry in oil for 5 minutes.

Add sugar and cook till it is completely melted.

Add tamarind and mix well.

Add lemon juice and all the spices.

Cook for 5 minutes, continuously stirring.

Remove from fire and bring to room temperature.

Store in the fridge until consumed.

98 CHILLI PINEAPPLE PICKLE

A tropical pickle. Pineapple pickle is easy to make and not only is it tasty but very versatile too.

Ingredients

1 ripe pineapple, skin removed and diced
1 tsp cumin seeds
1 tsp nigella seeds
1 tsp fennel seeds
1 tsp yellow mustard seeds
¼ tsp fenugreek seeds
1 tbsp ginger–garlic paste
⅓ cup sugar
¼ cup water
¼ tsp black salt
1 tsp salt

½ tsp red chilli flakes
1 tbsp white vinegar

Method

In a pan, dry-roast cumin, nigella, fenugreek, mustard and fennel seeds for 2 minutes and coarsely grind them.

In a pan, heat pineapple, add ginger–garlic paste and cook for 2–3 minutes.

Add sugar, salt and water, and cook for 10 minutes covered with a lid on medium heat.

Add the rest of the seasoning and 1 tsp of the coarsely ground spice mix and vinegar.

Cook for 2–3 minutes and remove from fire.

Store in a jar and refrigerate.

99 SWEET TAMARIND PICKLE

Tamarind is the fruit of a leguminous tree. It comes in the form of a bean-like pod, which is tangy and becomes sweet once it ripens. The fruit is used in cooking all over the world and also to make candies for children. I liberally use tamarind in my cooking as it enhances the taste of the recipes with its earthy, sweet and sour flavours. This is one of my favourite tamarind pickle recipes.

Ingredients

2 cups tamarind pulp
2 cups organic jaggery
2 tsp red chilli powder
1 tsp turmeric powder
1 tbsp salt

Method

Peel the dry skin of the tamarind and remove the seeds from the fruit.

Soak tamarind in a bowl full of hot water for 10 minutes.

In a pan, add jaggery and ½ cup of water to make a thick syrup.

Take a non-stick pan, add tamarind soaked in water and cook for 15 minutes, adding ¼ glass of water on medium heat until a thick mixture is obtained.

Add turmeric, salt and chilli powder and stir.

Adjust the seasoning if required.

Add the jaggery syrup through a sieve to filter out any particles.

Cook for 20 minutes on medium heat until the mixture becomes thick.

Transfer into a glass jar and seal it with its lid.

Refrigerate and consume within 1 month.

100 CHILLI GARLIC PICKLE

Garlic has great medicinal value and is extensively used all across the globe in cooking. This pickle can be eaten with breads, main courses, soups, meze, etc.

Ingredients

1 cup small bird's eye red chillies
1 cup garlic cloves
1 tbsp fennel seeds
1 tbsp cumin seeds
¼ tsp fenugreek seeds
1 tbsp black mustard seeds
1 tbsp coriander seeds
2 cups mustard oil
1½ tsp salt
½ tsp turmeric powder
½ cup distilled white vinegar

For tempering

1 tsp mustard seeds
2 sprigs curry leaves
8 garlic cloves
¼ tsp asafoetida

Method

Wash and dry the chillies. Slit them with a sharp knife without severing them.

Dry-roast the seeds and coarsely grind them.

Heat 2 cups of mustard oil to its smoking point.

Turn off the flame and bring the oil to room temperature.

Add garlic cloves and fry on medium heat till light golden brown.

Remove from oil and grind them coarsely in a blender.

In a pan, add slit chillies, salt, turmeric and coarsely ground seeds, and mix well.

Add fried garlic and stir in vinegar.

Use the same oil for tempering the cloves, mustard seeds, curry leaves and asafoetida.

Fry for about 1–2 minutes on low flame.

Pour the tempering with oil on the prepared pickle in a glass jar.

Mix well. Seal the jar with its lid.

Let the pickle ripen and sour for a week in the sun, shaking and stirring frequently.

Store in a cool, dark place until consumed.